MY LIFE AS EVA

GALLERY
BOOKS

An Imprint of Simon & Schuster, Inc.
1230 Avenue of the Americas
New York, NY 10020

First Gallery Books hardcover edition February 2017

GALLERY BOOKS and colophon are registered
trademarks of Simon & Schuster, Inc.

Certain names and characteristics have been
changed, whether or not so noted in the text.

For information about special discounts for bulk
purchases, please contact Simon & Schuster
Special Sales at 1-866-506-1949 or
business@simonandschuster.com.

The Simon & Schuster Speakers Bureau can bring
authors to your live event. For more information
or to book an event, contact the Simon & Schuster
Speakers Bureau at 1-866-248-3049 or visit our
website at www.simonspeakers.com.

Interior design and illustrations by Jane Archer
(janearcher.nyc | @psbellanyc)

Manufactured in the United States of America

10 9 8 7 6 5 4 3 2 1

Library of Congress Cataloging-in-Publication Data
is available.

ISBN 978-1-5011-4666-4
ISBN 978-1-5011-4674-9 (ebook)

MY LIFE AS EVA

the struggle is real

eva gutowski

GALLERY BOOKS

NEW YORK   LONDON   TORONTO   SYDNEY   NEW DELHI

Contents

Introduction: FETUS EVA

've always been the type of girl to believe in fantasies—almost a bit too much. Growing up, I managed to bury my head in any books I could get my hands on. Maybe it was because I enjoyed the immense benefits of bettering my education . . . or because my grandma used to pay me a quarter every time I read a book as a kid. Either way, it turned me into a total romantic, and a crazy, wild dreamer. Books took my mind to a place I'd never been before, and a place that, at the time, I thought I could never go.

Truth is, books are really all I had sometimes. My family couldn't afford to get me all the things I wanted, but one thing that's for certain is that they always made sure I had books to read. Honestly, going to the bookstore when I was a teen was practically more exciting than going to Disneyland. My grandma used to take me down the street to the (now closed) popular bookstore and just wait at the cafe for me while I searched and searched for the perfect books to buy.

I've always been completely enthralled by stories I could only get my hands on when I opened a book. Stories are my everything. Sometimes I ask myself why. Why do I fall in love with these stories and characters? Why do I fall in love with these stories so easily? Maybe it's just that: *love*. I'm a hopeless romantic. I believe in magic. I believe in fairy tales existing somewhere out there in this world, and I love the idea of the kind of fairy tale you'd read about in a book happening to little old me.

Books made me see the world a little differently. They made me think that getting my first kiss would be magical, that I

1

could go all the way until my sophomore year of high school before finding out I was actually a princess, and that maybe someday an owl would show up at my window and take me away to hone my skills as a wizard.

None of which happened.

However, a few good things came out of reading, like my love for writing. And story-telling. Growing up, I wrote every single night in composition journals that cost seventy-five cents, and stashed them under my bed hoping my parents wouldn't find them (they totally probably did).

[Side note: Mom, if you're reading this and actually did find my journals—please just lie to me and say you didn't. I will actually *die* if you tell me you read them!]

I wrote songs, poems, and scripts, and even attempted to write a few novels . . . all of which I could never find time between schoolwork to finish. I guess I just wanted to create a few stories of my own.

It's been a few years now, and even though I never finished any of the books I started writing when I was growing up, I told myself that if I could just finally finish *one* someday, I'd be happy. I didn't know how it would happen, or when, or what this magical finished book would even say inside its pages, but I knew if I worked hard enough, eventually I'd see my name on a shiny, glossy book cover. With my name as the author.

So here is my book. A book by me— Eva!

Wow, twenty-one years old and already a published author?

DAAAAAMN, EVA!

As I finish the writing of this book, it's 2016, and senior year of college is approaching, although I'm taking a year hiatus due to my YouTube commitments. It's been a long journey of growing up, and even though I'm still not nearly close to done with growing, I have a lot of stories that are itching to be told.

Now I must warn you that I'm nowhere near an expert on typical how-to things: like, here is a list of things I can't teach you . . .

 How to bake a cake that doesn't come from a box.

Seriously, why would you bake a cake from scratch when they have literal cake in a box . . . like, just add water and an egg. It ain't that serious.

 How to do a fishtail braid.

Look, I've been taught how to fishtail three times and still can't do it on my own.

 How to get your cat out of a tree.

My cat can't climb trees. Her legs are too little. That's a good thing.

Expert advice on how to be the perfect human is not my forte. However, I can tell you this:

You're going to go through a lot of different stages in your life. Literally, I've been through it all. From the emo stage to the scene stage, from crying all night from desperate sadness to crying all night from helpless laughter.

And life won't be easy at some points, but you have to realize life isn't supposed to be easy. If everyone lived their lives with no sadness, no pain, and nothing going absolutely and completely wrong, how would we appreciate the simple but amazing moments? You have to push through the bad times to get to the magical times, and I can tell you that my life, though not always perfect, is pretty freaking magical.

So if you're looking for a guide to making you "cool" or popular, or if you want to learn how to do the perfect French-braided topknot or contoured cheekbones, this may not be the book for you. I still can't fishtail-braid my hair and I've been taught like a hundred times (yes, I know I said three, but it's really more like over a hundred!). Instead, this book is all about teaching you how to love yourself for exactly who you are. Being okay with what your momma gave you and rocking it.

It's also all about figuring out who you want to be. I mean, trust me, I had no idea—literally *no idea*—who I was in high school, but I did know *who* I wanted to be and *what* type of person I wanted to grow up to be. I had dreams, visions, and goals. Just like I know you do too!

The thing that got me through growing up was being excited for all the possibilities my life could have if I only worked hard and dreamed big. So I dreamed extremely big. I made lists late at night and mood boards and thought of every possible way to make life my own. By the end of this book, I know you're going to feel a wave of motivation tingling through your body. *That's* what I needed growing up—constant pushes to keep me motivated and keep me dreaming. Which is why I'm going to tell you a lot of embarrassing stories and interesting stories about my life, because I feel like the only way to let you know it's going to be okay is to fill you in on all the crazy shiz I've been through so you KNOW it's gonna be okay. Literally, I've been through a lot. I had a lot of obstacles when I was younger. I overcame them, and I made life mine, and I'm going to help you make your life yours.

This is a journey of my life to guide you through your own. It's a reflection of my own mistakes, best moments, and weirdest moments that I want to let you in on.

So here's what I will attempt to teach you:

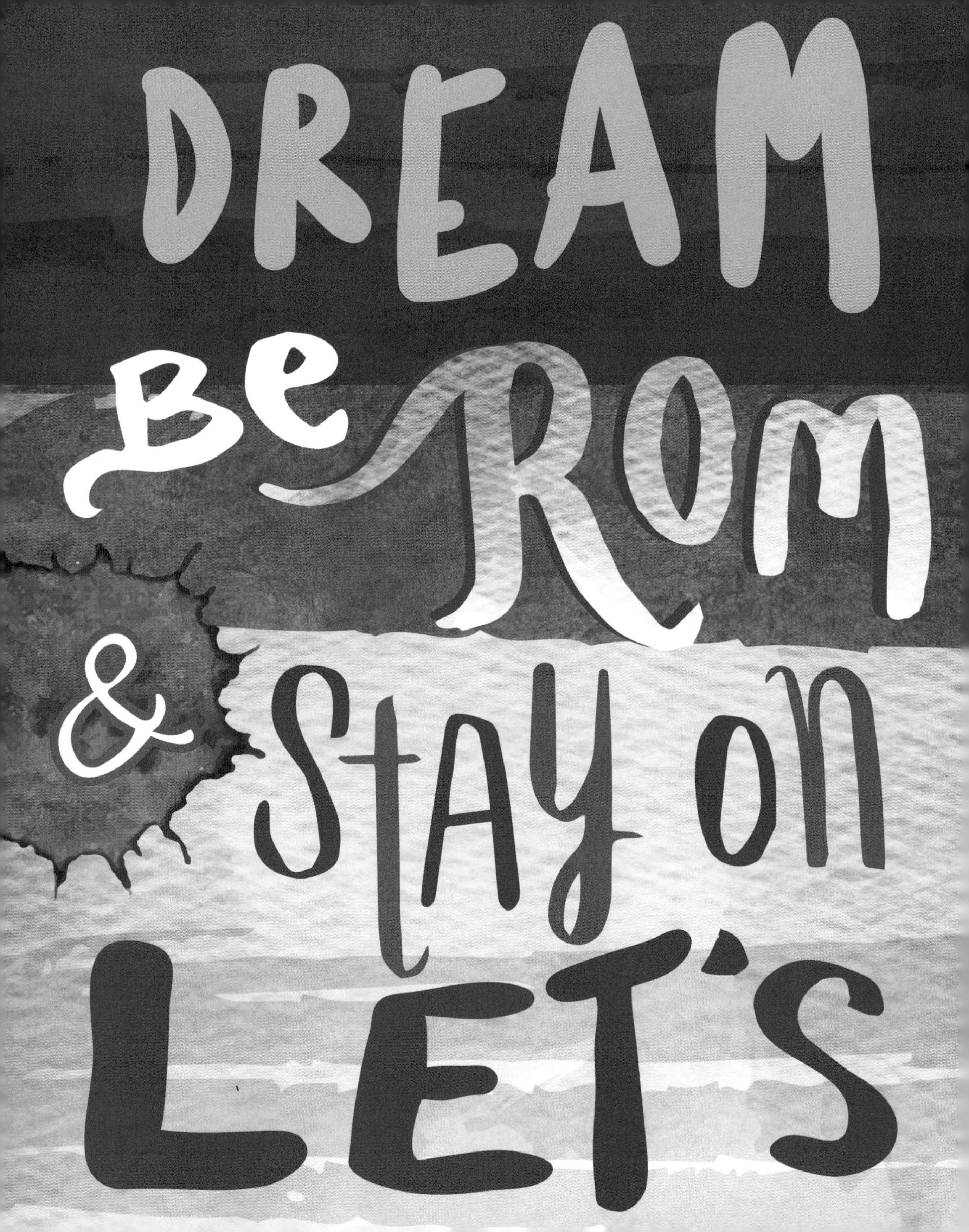
DREAM
Be Rom
& Stay on
LET'S

BIG Antic

YOUR PATH GO!

xo
Eva

FETUS EVA'S GUIDE to GETTING THROUGH THINGS: LISTS

This book is going to show you a lot of ways to get through things, but the number one thing you should always do is MAKE A LIST.

Here are some of the lists I made when I was growing up:

Cute boys
Names for future children
People I want to work for
Foods I hate

Making these lists is what got me through all the bad times. I went through a period in my life where I was crying in my room for hours about a lot of things.

I'll get into all the details later, but basically, I was going through some pretty negative things and I let them get the best of me. They consumed me for the longest time, and I became extremely depressed. So much in my life felt out of my hands, and overall, I think the thing I was most affected by was the idea that my life would never amount to anything I dreamed of it being.

I could have easily let depression win. But I didn't.

One of the reasons I was sad at that time was because I wanted to act but couldn't, because my family had no money for acting classes or the time or ability to take me on auditions, so I thought I'd never be able to be an actress and I was getting older every day (you know how every day that goes by when you're a teen can be excruciatingly *longgggg* when you are no closer to your dreams!) and nothing was helping me get closer to my goals.

But there's always a way to fix something—even if it's not an immediate solution. That's where my lists came in.

I realized I couldn't just drop everything and become an actress the next day . . . so I made a list instead. This list was:

MAYBE I WANT TO BE AN ACTRESS, BUT IF I CAN'T, THIS IS WHAT I WANT TO BE

○ A psychologist or therapist or school counselor (no way could I ever be a psychiatrist if I had to pass all that math they make you do in medical school)

○ A teacher

○ A professional surfer

○ A photographer

○ Oprah

○ Editor in chief of *Seventeen* magazine or *Teen Vogue*

○ A film director

WOW

Looking at this list now is kind of amazing, and if you know me from my videos, you can probably figure out why, right?

Because I'm already doing most of the jobs on my list!

I'm writing this book that's full of advice that I hope will help you and teach you. I love to surf. I take photos every day. I direct and edit my own videos.

Okay, so I'm not Oprah—but who else is? LOL.

Not long ago, I found another list that I wrote out with multicolored pens on a piece of computer paper. This list really makes me laugh:

THINGS I WANT TO BUY OR HAVE WHEN I GROW UP AND HAVE MY DREAM JOB AND CAN AFFORD TO BUY OR HAVE THEM

- A white Siberian husky with one blue eye
- A hanging wicker chair that swings around
- A Bugatti Veyron (but only to rent and only to drive to my high school reunion)
- A bed with a round mattress bed (um, where was I supposed to get the sheets???)
- A really gorgeous and expensive Teavana teapot
- Sliding French doors
- An outdoor bathtub
- A house with a living room that has a kind of indoor creek with lots of pebbles and flowing water and fish swimming around in it, like an underground fish tank (I saw this in a magazine and thought it was amazing)
- A spiral staircase
- Tickets to travel the world. Especially to Greece
- A haircut so my hair looks like I want my hair to look, like AnnaLynne McCord's did on 90210, because hers is so cool. One day it's like flowing California girl and then the next day it's all wavy and scrunchy. She has some good hair going on!
- Oprah's job
- A stylish baby
- My own clothing line. With basic pieces that are flowing and peasant-style, sort of like Greek boho
- The ability to write a book!!!

#GOALS

Believe in Yourself

SO GET LISTING!

SCHOOL

HEY YOU'RE CUTE COME KISS ME.

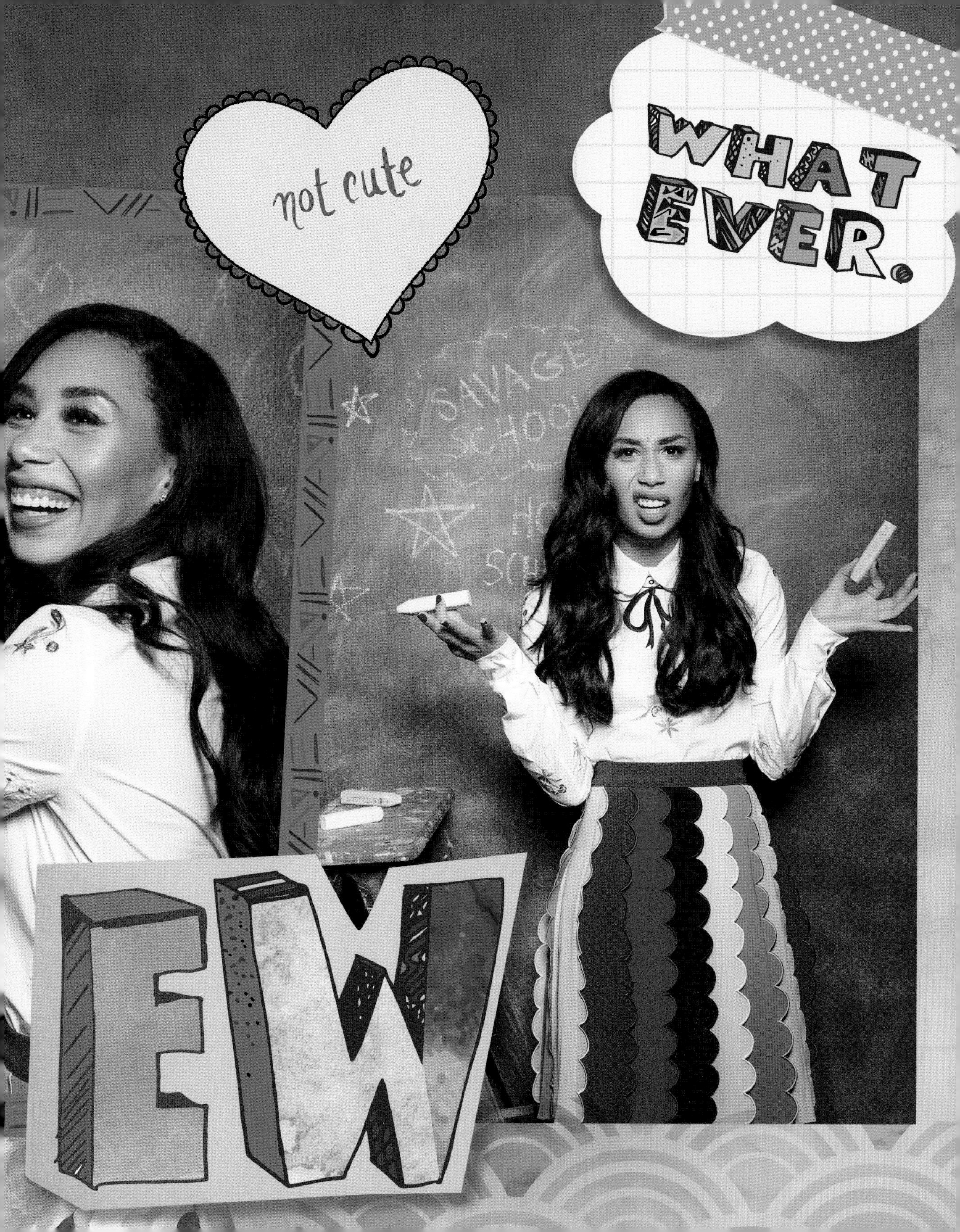
not cute
WHAT EVER.
SAVAGE SCHOOL
EW

CHAPTER 1

The Truth About
HIGH SCHOOL

High school for me was overall a good time. Despite some run-ins with bullies, some pretty intense heartbreaks, and some pretty deep and sometimes scary moments (don't worry—read on and I'll tell you all about them!), I had fun—and made it out alive. And despite all the times I wondered what in the holy guacamole nacho chips my teachers were trying to get me to do sometimes, I learned a lot in school. Not just about the subjects we were taught. About me, Eva.

Honestly, however sucky a lot of parts of high school may be, it's so necessary for teaching you how to survive in the **real** world. I swear I am so confident now in so many new ways, and I would never be if it weren't for getting rejected by nearly every boy I loved in high school. Seriously rejected badly. Once, I had a crush on my best friend and gave him a chocolate rose on Valentine's Day and asked him to be my valentine and he said no. Like . . . WTF. K, thanks!

High school, like life, isn't meant to be easy. Honestly if high school had been easy for me, I'd have been scared, because then that would have meant that I peaked when I was just a teenager and my life as Eva would have been all downhill from there.

Life has ups and downs, and life also has a really funny way of working itself out.

Especially in high school, you sometimes think it's the end of the flipping world just because so-and-so saw a text you sent about how cute they were, or how you'll never recover from falling on your face at a school assembly. Maybe someone's trying to get you to do something sketchy and you know you don't want to, but you also don't know how to say no.

I always tell people to be bold and courageous about the choices they are making **right now**. Right in this moment. People think it's the end of the world sometimes, and they're afraid to say how they really feel for fear of losing someone . . . even if that person literally sucks.

Growing up, I always knew what was right and what was wrong for me, but I had to become fearless in the art of saying YES and HELL NO. Once I could do that, it was a great feeling knowing that I could take my life into my own hands.

High school is crazy, and you'll make wrong decisions and a lot of right decisions, so don't worry too much about that. All you have to worry about is staying true to yourself and keeping positive vibes in your life. Listen—we don't have time for bad influences up in here!

And there's gonna be people that literally suck, yet for some psycho reason we don't know how to get them out of our lives. That's another art—the art of saying goodbye.

Goodbye doesn't always mean goodbye forever. Sometimes it means "I am tired of the way you make me feel, and until you fix yourself, I have to be selfish and go my own way for me to be happy."

There will come many times when you have to let someone go out of your life because they're dragging you down and causing you pain! Bullies, friends that do you dirty, boys who decide to crush your heart—don't be afraid to surround yourself with only positive people, and don't be afraid to tell someone goodbye.

Show people that you deserve to be treated with respect one time, and they always come around if they care. And if they don't care enough to come back, there's your answer for if they should even be in your life!

And most of all in high school, have fun. GO TO THINGS. Wear colorful school T-shirts. Invite someone to a school dance. Don't convince yourself that staying home is what you really want. Please please please don't miss out on all the fun— because trust me, what is being offered to you IS fun!

Basically, to sum it up: Don't worry too much about the Pythagorean theorem. Unless you are going to be a math teacher, you will NEVER use it. You will use all the life skills, though, so make sure to pay attention to the weird ecosystem of high school that's buzzing around you.

FRESHMAN FOLLIES

Ah, freshman year. The start of it all. Picture this: Little Eva, all of five foot four, brown hair, yellowish complexion, DEVIL WEARS PRADA T-shirt. I loved screamo music, went to music festivals, got caught in a mosh pit, and had a best friend that dyed her hair teal and preferred for everyone to ditch her real last name and changed it to "Tea." I ended up falling in love with a blond boy (go figure), and was in some pretty cool plays, where I got to play the role of a ballerina, a German girl . . . and a tree. I also joined the dance team, and that got me kicked in the face in front of my entire school, which was then filmed and uploaded to YouTube. I guess that was a sign that I would be embarrassing myself a lot on the internet in the future.

Freshman year was filled with a lot of hard times. It was the first time all the pressure at home really got to me, and even though school life was all right, at home I was really, really sad.

Nonetheless, I got through freshman year, and now that I look back, a lot of the moments that happened in this . . . let's not call it golden, but more like . . . bronze . . . or more like rusty year . . . were pretty hilarious. Let me share with you some of my favorite moments.

My First Bully

High school is easy to survive—if you know the right way to handle all the crazy things that get thrown at you. Trust me—crazy things *will* get thrown at you. Literally and figuratively. Like I once got an empty milk carton pelted at me in home ec. By my ex-boyfriend. But that's another story.

So, *ahem*!

Picture me on my very first day of high school. Little fetus Eva. There I was, clip-in Claire's extensions and all, feeling as confident as ever. My family had scraped up enough money to take me "back-to-school shopping": when you are not part of the upper-middle class of upper-middle-class Orange County, the event may as well be labeled a national holiday. I was particularly excited about my new, clearance-rack white Hollister shorts and purple V-neck top from Kmart, but I needed to add an Eva touch to the look, so I dug through my sock dresser and slipped on my purple soccer socks from a team I'd been on when I was twelve. I walked out to grab my backpack and showed my mom my sweet look. She told me to turn around and take the socks off. Apparently, I looked ridiculous. So I switched my socks to a more conservative white pair, packed my purple socks into my backpack, climbed into my grandma's old gray truck, and off we went to school at a rapid thirty-five miles per hour. That was always the appropriate grandma speed.

Finally, I saw the green-and-gold sign with my high school's name on it as it whisked past me, and suddenly my grandma was driving away and I was climbing the steps to my new home for the next four years. I made a quick change in the bathroom into my soccer socks and headed out the door to find my first class. Now, entering high school on that first day was scary enough, but it was just when I was getting familiar with all the new ins and outs of how things worked that I got familiar . . . with Candy.

There I was, a scrawny, noodlelike, purple-soccer-socked freshman girl, just trying to find an empty seat in Spanish class. I finally sat down and looked around, yet I suddenly realized that something was off. Everyone's eyes weren't looking around as well. Nope—they were looking at freaking lil' old *me*. I started having that feeling where it feels like hot soup and stones are being piled up in your abdomen, and suddenly the girl next to me flipped her perfectly blown-out hair and whispered, "Oh my gosh, you're Eva? Oh. Okay, so . . . Candy wants to jump you. She's been looking for you and she wants to beat you up."

Um, excuse me? *What?* Hold on let me explain myself . . . Hi, my name is Eva and I haven't met a girl named Candy in my entire life. Also, I spend my days eating Push Pops and riding my bike around my neighborhood. I can't think of a single thing I've done to create beef with someone. Can you imagine? I never fought with anybody in my entire life. And never will! Like, that's not my thing.

So I was thinking, first of all, Who is this Candy? and second of all, Hi, I'm just me, Eva, lowly freshman in high school land, and I'm super confused! Why would someone with the sweet name of Candy want to jump me? Eva, what the hell did you do? Was I wearing the same shirt as her? I didn't even know who she was! All I knew was that I hadn't done anything wrong.

A minute later, I was contemplating all the life choices I'd made in the past forty-eight hours and one of my classmates pointed her out. There she was. Candy, sitting not in her seat, but on her desk, with a bunch of boys huddled around her. A senior, of course. She was a lot shorter than me, but she looked strong. Think a bulldog . . . with lots of crazy red hair.

OMG, what do I do? I was trying not to look at Candy, but I saw her out of the corner of my eye. She was joking with her guy squad and I was hearing laughs and loud whispers. My thoughts were racing. I thought about all my options—you know, like crawling into a trash can and never coming out (some are probably still clean), crying to a teacher (no way, social suicide), or running out of school to get a black belt in karate like overnight (um, not very realistic) . . . or maybe how about just being me, Eva, and finding out what was really going on and dealing with the situation.

Long story short, I got a piece of paper out of my notebook and quickly wrote Candy a nice note, even though my hand was kind of shaking, and I had a strong urge to poop out of my chest really badly:

Hi Candy.

My name's Eva and everyone's saying you want to jump me and I don't know why. I'm sure you're a nice person. I don't know anything about you. Can we talk about what's going on? I don't know what's going on—I don't know who you are, to be honest. and I don't know what I did wrong. but can you please tell me before you freaking beat me up? I'm sure you're a cool person.

Thanks. Eva

I was scared as hell of what was going to happen. I mean, I was either going to get beat up just because, or I was going to get beat up after Candy read my note of me trying to explain the situation and her not believing me. Who knew, I might even hand her the note and she'd throw it away. Either way, I had to make a move. I was trying to talk myself into being brave and suddenly I looked up and Candy had SLID INTO THE SEAT NEXT TO ME. She was leaning on the desk looking at me like she was a lion in a jungle and I was a rabbit that had just broken its leg and was basically just awaiting my imminent death. I gulped and passed her the note as she glared at me. She read it, and then I saw her shoulders relax and she quickly started writing me back.

This is what happened to make her so mad . . . Apparently this guy, Ricky, who I'd had a sort of fling with in the summer, was mad because I didn't like him anymore. So naturally, he told Candy that I had CALLED HER FAT. Even though I'd never seen Candy in my ENTIRE LIFE and would never talk about someone like that!

He wanted me to get punished for not liking him. WHO DOES THAT?

As soon as I read Candy's note back, everything clicked. I immediately started explaining to her how I'd met Ricky over the summer, the story of what had happened between us (basically nothing), and how he turned out to be kind of crazy, how I would never in my life say the things he said to her. She believed me. Turns out, she didn't really trust Ricky either. We became friends, and Ricky became irrelevant AF, and for the rest of senior year and even after Candy graduated, she always made sure to say hi when she saw me.

I could have done without the drama on the first day of high school, that's for sure, but it definitely taught me a huge lesson in dealing with drama the right way.

WHAT YOU REALLY LEARN IN HIGH SCHOOL

Looking back, I realized that, guess what! That lesson I learned that day in Spanish class on my very first day of high school was a lot more important in a lot of ways than anything I ever read about in any of my schoolbooks.

What I really learned:

- You can't do anything about the Rickys of the world, who have their own agendas and can't manage their own feelings without needing to hurt someone else.

- The only way to respond to the Rickys of the world is by being honest and standing your ground for what you believe in. Most people think they can walk all over you because, to be honest, a lot of us are scared to stick up for ourselves and have never been in a situation where we really had to. Once you show someone that not only do you know how you deserve to be treated, but that you won't stand for someone trying to treat you wrong, they'll never test you again. There's ways to handle crazy situations by just being true to who you are, and explaining your feelings well.

In other words:

I think the real purpose of high school is about learning social skills. Learning how to interact with people—both good and bad. Learning how to talk to boys. Learning how to get rejected by people . . . many, many times. Learning how to deal with hurt. Learning how to deal with happiness too. And it sucks sometimes, because obviously nobody's life is perfect, and everyone—even the popular and charismatic people you think have it all figured out—goes through their own battles. High school is made to seem like it's all about getting your grades to be perfect in order to succeed in life, but in reality, all the reading, writing, and finding of the letter x in math problems is just filler stuff while you learn the important lessons: *life* lessons.

I had to read so many books in AP language, and looking back years later, it's not the perfect diction, the use of symbolism, or the "tone" I remember. It's the long nights I spent slaving trying to get a rough draft written by first period the next day, or the way the books made me feel about life, or the friends I made in the class. Honestly, half the books I wrote essays on, I didn't even finish reading (sorry, Mrs. Thomas!).

That's what you have to experience—emotional intelligence.

So here's what I've learned about keeping up in school:

 Don't expect to be good at everything. The point is, you have to try.

Some people really thrive on learning about topics they know they'll probably never need to know about for the rest of their lives (Brent Rivera). That's cool. For *them*. For me, some topics were really, really tough. Like math. Like the Pythagorean theorem. Like finding *f* of *x*. Please, just make it stop!

But here's the thing about subjects you can't stand or can't get no matter how hard you try (seriously, f you, algebra!). Yeah, it sucks, I get it—but that's not the point. The point is way beyond learning how to do a stupid math problem. To be honest, teachers aren't looking for you to shine in every subject you're thrown into. They don't expect you to become a rocket scientist after a simple geometry lesson. They are just looking to see you put in the effort and just simply **try**.

Teachers know that 99.9999 percent of students will NOT be good at everything. It's the rare student who is, so expecting otherwise is ridiculous. Too often, people put pressure on you to be perfect and fail at nothing, but what they forget to remind you is that they're only trying to test you to see how you handle something. I know it's hard being in a class when there's a kid who is just slaying the game, never studies, and somehow finishes his in-class assignments in record speed, and then there you are, literally staring at your calculator wondering how to even turn it on.

Are you going to try anyway? Yes, you are.

That's it. Just try it out! Try your hardest to understand something, and if you just can't, that's OKAY. I mean, as you might have figured out already, I literally suck at math. I've tried. I've done all I can. My brain just can't get good at it. It all started back in the third grade when I was first learning my multiplication times tables. Virtually all the other kids in class were already onto long division and there I was, still practicing my freaking 9 x 4 = whatever. (I honestly still couldn't even tell you what that answer is without writing it out first!) My teacher worked me so hard because I wasn't getting it as quickly as the other kids—so hard that she even made me cry in class. Did that help? Of course not. I just couldn't make my brain work as fast as the other kids and I didn't know why. Fast-forward to high school, and I had to repeat algebra twice. I still couldn't get it!

By that time, thank goodness I had some more forgiving teachers that tried their best to encourage me instead of make me cry in the classroom. It was around this time that I came to terms with myself. Listen, Eva, I told myself, you just cannot figure out math. You can't. So what if you always hear people say, "Nobody 'can't' do something; they're just giving up." Okay, well then, you are "giving up" at being good at math . . . .

I'm kidding. Sort of! I knew I couldn't really give up, because I still had to try hard enough to pass the class and graduate. I had to keep on trying.

Maybe this is bad advice, but it's something I definitely needed to hear in high school. Don't beat yourself up for not being good at every single subject. We weren't put on this earth to get A-pluses for eighteen straight years. We were put on this earth to find out what we're good at, what we love to do, and then figure out how we can channel that into making the world a better place. Teachers know that, but rarely do they let YOU know that.

So if you find yourself sucking at a subject and hating its guts for a consecutive twelve years—hi, Pythagoras, remember me?—just remember that you only need to be good enough to pass the class. Focus instead on being the best you can be at what you're truly good at. And focus just as much on finding what you love to do, not on getting stressed out on something you hate doing and that you know for sure is not going to be part of your future.

 It's not about what you learn from a textbook—it's what you learn from you.

The best thing that comes out of a challenge is finding out how YOU handle it. Keep in mind, we don't all handle challenges the same. Some people cry, some people get angry, some people get motivated, and some people get lazy. And sometimes the way we handle challenges isn't exactly the best way. If I had a dollar for every time I went through a challenge just in schoolwork alone, I'd literally be able to buy an island in the Bahamas. It was FRUSTRATING. I wanted to give up so many times. But how would you ever know how to handle a challenge if you never had to go through any?

It's not about the dumb word problems that are thrown at you—because let's be real honest here: those word problems are meant to be ridiculous. If Sally had three lemons and gave two away, but replanted a tree that blooms in August, what does she have? A VERY SWEET HEART BUT VERY CRAPPY LEMONADE AND NOW SHE HAS TO WAIT UNTIL AUGUST FOR HER LEMONADE TO BE BETTER. DAMN.

High school is not about solving the dumb word problems of the world. It's about learning how to deal with *failing* the word problems a bunch of times and finding out what you need to do to finally get them right.

The long nights you'll endure in college, work, and just life in general, trying to solve something that seems impossible, will be a whole lot easier when you're already a pro at finding out what works for you. And that means learning to push past the struggles with classwork and homework that, if you're like me, are going to push all of your very worst buttons.

And you'll never really know how to handle challenges until the pressure is on, like getting and keeping a solid GPA to participate in sports, or being admitted to a college on your top-ten list, for example.

That's why high school is the perfect place to learn who you are in the world of challenges.

Don't let but-what-about-college scare you!

Not everyone is meant for college. Not everyone is meant for a top-ranked school. Many, many people in this world do very, very well with the choices they make about what kind of post–high school education or training is best for them.

Everyone wants to make college out to seem like this very important, very prestigious, and very scary place, and if you don't get straight A's in high school, then not only will you not get into college, but you will also be a massive weirdo who is most definitely deciding to f up their life and become a hobo. Not true!

It's not about the grades. It's about finding out about yourself!

In high school, they push everything on you for a reason, whether you believe that or not at the time. The reason is so you find out what you like and what you hate and what you're good at and what you might be good at, and, hopefully, what you love love love more than anything. And if you love it, it's what you'll do or become when you grow up!

I have to tell you that I didn't get good grades in a lot of my classes.

Basically like C's and even sometimes D's. Could I have gotten better grades if I'd studied a lot more? Maybe. Okay, *probably*! When I was growing up, I read so much, so many books, probably every single book in the young adult section of the library at school. But in high school I must confess I discovered SparkNotes. They really helped me. Should I have read the whole book? Well, yeah! Would it have helped my development and my appreciation of literature? Well, yeah again! Did I think it would affect my life when I was twenty-five? Well, no! I guess that's kind of cheating, but I knew I wasn't strong enough to do really well in my honors English class, even though I liked to write a lot and was really good at it. But I'd gotten to the point in my life where I was too busy to spend time reading *Catch-22*, and if the book didn't seem interesting to me, I wouldn't read the whole thing.

Maybe if other books we had to read in English were as good as *The Great Gatsby*, things would have been different. I *loved* that book. I wrote essays that were just the bomb on it. It had the best influence on me, more than anything else I've ever read, and I'm sure if I'd read all the other books I was supposed to have read they would have influenced me too. *Gatsby* just got to me. It made me think about what life was like in the 1920s, and it had so many messages in it, like about wanting something so badly that you're never going to have, and then realizing that what you thought you wanted wasn't worth the dreams you put on it.

Like, be careful what you wish for, you know?

And don't mess up like Gatsby did. He turned out to be so stupid!

radiate positive vibes

I AM SURROUNDED BY IDIOTS.

FRESHMAN YEAR

CHAPTER 2

Glo-Up Level, FRESHMAN STYLE

et's consider freshman year the year of some of my biggest glo-up fails. I didn't know what I was doing, but the worst part was I THOUGHT I knew what I was doing. I shopped at Hot Topic on a weekly basis. I chopped my hair into a weird uneven bowl cut, which I attempted to even out with cheap clip-in synthetic hair extensions. I didn't know what makeup was aside from what I managed to get my hands on from my mom's collection, and I thought somehow this outfit would be a good idea.

I think I just really wanted to fit in, you know, with my lack of friends and everything.

This is also around the time that I got my first camera. It was a $20 webcam that mounted to my dad's laptop. I thought I was a photographer and made all these intricate, highly saturated edits of webcam pictures.

I added them all to Facebook and decided to start what I assumed was a photography business, which I called

This is how I used to edit in high school . . . I guess you can say not much has changed since then! I still do love saturation!

"AEG," or "Adorkable Eva Gutowski." Artistic. But you know, I must have been in a great headspace when creating this album in Facebook because even the location was artsy—"Taken at the center of Eva's mind." Wtf was I thinking.

EVA'S EYEBROWS FRESHMAN YEAR = *Nonexistent*

So the whole world is about eyebrow game being strong these days, but in high school I had barely any brows to work with. My eyebrows never grew in lush or thick, like my mom's. They grew in like my dad's—sparse and all over the place. At the time, I barely had a lip gloss to my name, so filling in my brows wasn't even an option or thought. The worst moment was when I went to the local wax spot to get them cleaned up for a school dance (when they really didn't need it. I just felt like going to feel normal), and the lady goes, "STOP PLUCKING YOUR BROWS! LET THEM BREATHE AND THEY WILL GROW!" Excuse me, lady, but I HAVE NEVER TOUCHED MY BROWS. I WAS CURSED WITH THEM! She didn't believe me!

They still look like that. Trust me, there's nothing I can do!

EVA'S POLKA-DOT NAIL POLISH HOW-TO WALK-THRU

I learned how to master the art of polka-dot nail polish, and was so proud of this that I spent literally all of freshman year to college sporting different combos of polka-dot nail polish. I'm not embarrassed by this though. My nails always looked cool.

All you have to do is polish your nails whatever color you want your base to be. Put on a topcoat. Let it dry really well. Then use the brush that comes in the polish bottle, or even a Q-tip (if it's not too thick), and dip it into another color. Hold this over your nail and let the other color plop on in a drip so it's a circle. It takes just a few tries to get it right, and then you might find yourself as obsessed with it as I was at the time, because it's so much fun to experiment with different color combos.

I still love my nails to be long and manicured, and I get tips put on all the time. Except when I'm going to go surfing. Boards and long nails do not mix!

EVA'S HAIR HELL

Since my hair was now a lopped-off bowl-cut mess (note to self: don't get a $15 haircut . . . . and don't keep going back because it's cheap), I had to deal with my curly mess of Puerto Rican hair not being able to be pulled into a proper ponytail without looking like a ball of brown macaroni and cheese. I had to improvise. Luckily for me, my grandma had a perfectly tangled curly-hair-extension ponytail that was three shades too light for my hair color and was also missing the ponytail part. Let's call it the poop pony, because it resembled horse poop extremely close-up. Are you thinking what I'm thinking? Yes, I found a way to fashion that ball of reddish-brown hair to my head every single day for months. To make things even more stylish, I straightened just the top half of my hair and pulled it into a comb-over and fastened it with a barrette. Chic.

Hair was not my specialty back then,

and it still isn't. However, I tried as hard as I could to find what exact style my hair needed back then. Since my poop pony was getting too tangled for me to keep using it, I needed to move on. So, I cut myself some stylish straight bangs and threw the hair I cut off into my DRESSER. I still have no idea why.

The bangs weren't doing me justice and they were giving me a lot of acne due to the hair product rubbing on my face since I had to use so much Blue Magic and hair sheen to keep my hair straight through the day, so I ended up settling for my bowl cut and pushing the bangs to the side for the rest of the year.

If I could go back, I would have treated my natural hair a lot better. I think my hair failed so much simply because I kept messing with it to make it do things it didn't want to do. Hair has FEELINGS! I kept making my hair try to be a silky sleek Norwegian supermodel's when it really wanted to be a 1970s mixed hippie woman's . . . or a mushroom. Regardless, here is what I should have done with my hair:

Not straightened it unless I really wanted to for a special occasion! *If your hair isn't naturally straight, maybe don't try to fry it every single day to be straight. Natural is beautiful! Curls are gorgeous! Learn how to rock your own God-given style!*

Worn more buns and pulled-back styles. *Not every day has to be Victoria's Secret–model day.*

Moisturized! *For God's sake, woman, hair needs moisture love too! I wish I had slathered my hair in coconut oil growing up, because maybe now I'd have long gorgeous curly hair like Zendaya. But I knew that if I had used oils or really anything with any type of moisturizing qualities, my hair wouldn't have been straight like a white girl's, so I avoided any type of those products. This left my hair dry as a bone—bad idea.*

Stopped getting bad haircuts. *I know $17.99 sounds like a bargain at the time, but you pay more for the emotional turmoil of the messed-up haircut in the long run. Plus, it will end up costing you more because you've got to pay someone to undo the damage.*

EVA'S ZIT CENTRAL

At the time, like I said, my skin wasn't being too sexy. It was dry and flaky, and had a ton of acne scars. The sucky thing about my skin back then was that I would get pimples and then they would go down in a week, but the marks would stay FOREVER. (This is totally normal and totally annoying. It's called hyperpigmentation. Or hyper-hellacious.) The marks kept building up and nothing I tried was

helping to get rid of them. I was feeling extremely unconfident about my skin, especially because almost all the other girls in school had perfect skin. This was something I was always thinking about. Luckily, near the end of my freshman year, my grandma came to the rescue and helped me out with some makeup that covered up the worst of the marks without clogging up my pores.

Things I Should Have Done for My Skin

So, yeah, I had a typical case of teenage acne when I was in high school. Yes, I should have seen a dermatologist, but my family could barely afford for me to see a doctor (which you'll read about in Chapter 11), and so I never saw one.

I think part of the problem was that there were four of us living in a very small apartment and we all had stuff and stress and it got really messy and the number one priority wasn't making it all beauti-

ful and sparkling clean. We had laundry machines for our complex, but they were expensive and broken a lot of the time, and then you needed a stack of quarters, and it was hard to fit in all the sheets and pillowcases, and it was a real pain. I often would bring all my clothes to wash at my grandma's house, but her machine broke a lot too, so our laundry days weren't as frequent as they should have been.

And this is what I learned: It's a dirty world out there. Your face is gonna react to it, especially if you're tired. You need to wash your face every single night to get the day's grime off, especially if you wear makeup. And you need to wash your linens regularly to get the grime that you didn't wash off your face off, or else it gets on your pillow and ends up all over your face and it makes your skin look terrible.

Then there's everything else you touch. Like the desks at school, or tapping your pencils on your cheeks, or leaning up against your locker. Or what you touch on a plane. That's me, putting my head on the pillow, or falling asleep pressed up against the window shade, and then I wake up and think, OMG, Eva, how many people are doing that this many times a day, are they sanitizing all that sweat and disgustingness at all? No, they are not! So this is why you get off a plane and your skin is so bad—two hours later it's like I have like five pimples pop up out of nowhere just from touching everything. *Ewwww!*

Believe me when I say I tried every drugstore zit product that ever existed in the history of the world. I soon learned that these products often didn't do what they said they would—but at least they got me washing my face. One particular astringent, Clean & Clear, worked pretty well and I used it for five years straight. I didn't have a lot of luck with Proactiv, although some of my friends did, but that probably because I was too lazy and also couldn't afford it! But then one day we moved into a new apartment and the previous tenant had forgotten to change his address and I got a big package with his regular Proactiv items in it, and I thought, Well, Eva, this is a sign, so don't be so lazy! Too bad it still didn't help all that much.

Luckily, my skin gradually cleared up with time, although I still break out when I'm getting my period. And I am a lot more scrupulous about taking off my makeup and washing my face!

And you know what else I noticed? People who surf a lot and are in the ocean a lot have amazing skin. That's the secret every surfer will tell you. Chlorine in pools messes with your skin and dries it out, but the salt in the ocean is actually an exfoliant and gives you great skin. It lightens your hair and makes it all shiny and wavy. There's nothing better than that healthy glow you get after a workout, especially one in the ocean—it's better than all the makeup in the world.

Just don't follow my example if you go to the beach, TBH, because I don't wear sunscreen. I don't burn, except for when my nose peels. I know, I know. Someday I'll pay the price. Like the other day when I saw a brown sun spot on my arm. My bad!

EVA'S VAMPIRE TEETH

Growing up, I always had weird teeth. I had these two big teeth on each side of my face that were long and pointy—like a vampire's. In third grade, a girl actually (and I'm not kidding) convinced me that I was a vampire. Literally, I started writing in my journal to "document the journey to discovering my true vampire self." But back to the point: my teeth always bugged me. When I was around ten, I remember going to the orthodontist and hearing him say that to fix my smile, I'd need jaw surgery, braces for five years, and then veneers to even out my weird vampire teeth. Even at ten, I knew all that sounded super expensive, and extremely time-consuming. And painful. I figured, OKAY, so if I need to have braces for five years, let's throw them on right now while all my friends have them, so in high school I'll be all done with them and be HOT.

Nope.

My family was already working so hard just to pay the bills that there was no way they could take on paying for braces. It was the worst thing ever, because I wanted them so bad. And I *needed* them. It was honestly the only thing I ever really really really wanted.

I got through elementary school and junior high with my goofy teeth, because I figured I was still just a little kid and it was acceptable, but during freshman year of high school I stepped onto campus and it seemed like all of my fellow freaky-teeth friends had turned five years older overnight. EVERYONE seemed like they'd gotten their braces off, and yet there I was, still unbraced. It affected me so much that I would cry sometimes because of how different and juvenile I felt, walking around campus with my crazy "vampire fangs." I knew that someday, when I got older, I'd just have to get braces and fix my teeth myself, but until then I'd have to learn to love my unique teeth.

EVA'S DISCOVERY OF THE SECRET OF TRUE BEAUTY

One of the toughest things I struggled with during freshman year was just being comfortable in my own skin. It's normal. When you're growing up, it's hard being okay with who you are, especially when you see, no matter where you turn, images of girls you think are prettier or have better bodies or are more physically blessed than you. Let me be honest. I was not "blessed" with perfect eyebrows or perfectly big-but-not-too-big boobs. Or wavy long hair or perfect skin. I was blessed with some stringy-ass eyebrows, acne that would follow me to adulthood, and a body that resembled that of a twelve-year-old pre-pubescent boy on most days. I knew that!

But that didn't mean I couldn't love myself anyway.

I knew that even though my teeth were funny and my gums took up half my face, my smile was bright and warmed everyone up when I laughed. My smile was friendly and happy, and I loved that about myself more than any perfect set of pearly whites.

You'll never be more beautiful than you tell yourself you are. Than you believe you are. You need to believe that, even though there's days where you wish you looked different. You need to accept yourself! The glo-up happens with time and patience, but no glo-up can ever happen until you're ready to become a better version of YOU, not someone else you wish to look like.

And so even though freshman year I often looked like an overcooked Froot Loop, I knew that someday I would be pretty freaking hot, and all the boys in high school who thought I was a straight lost cause would learn to recognize it. I knew one day I'd be working what I've got. Everyone's "got it," in some way. You just have to find out how to work it!

But back then . . . I still looked weird.

I didn't quite know all the ins and outs of how to take care of myself in high school so I could avoid bad hair days, bad skin days, and more . . . but now I know a lot more! It's important to note that even though you could be given all the tips and tricks in the world, you're still going to have off days. I have a bad hair day almost daily. Like right now my edges are NOT laid. But I just don't care!

Not every day has to be a 10/10 banger when it comes to hair, fashion, and beauty. Just focus on what matters— and what matter is you feeling great. I feel pretty dang okay looking like a hermit crab missing a few legs.

And here is a very interesting lesson I learned from my friend Sam. About makeup. A lesson I wish I had learned back in freshman year.

I got in the habit of putting makeup on most school days and other days when I know I have to go out. (I don't care so much when I'm just going to be in the house or around people I know.) It's a nice habit, as my routine doesn't take very long, and it helps wake me up and get me out the door.

Anyway, I went to Hawaii with my friend Sam. I'm a pretty adventurous person by nature, and am happy to go camping in the woods for like twenty days straight, as long as I have my trusty makeup bag with me and a whole lot of deodorant. So there I was in Sam's house, planning to stay for a week, and as usual I'd put my makeup on first thing in the morning. On my third day there, we went for a nice long hike and then went back to his house and stretched out on the roof and the sun was shining and all that, and we were just relaxing and yakking away. He told me that one of his friends said he was only a 6.4 out of 10, and he got sad, and then I started saying nice things about his appearance to make him feel better. And then I teased him and asked him how he would rate me, and what didn't he like about my appearance, and he said, "Well, I kinda don't like that you wear so much makeup."

I was a bit taken aback, and asked him what he meant.

"I don't have any sisters, you know," he explained, "and my mom didn't wear makeup—basically I grew up on this island where no girls ever wear makeup here. It takes up too much time, and it's too hot. Besides, Eva, you don't need it and you are super beautiful without it, and if you go hiking or surfing you know it's gonna come off anyway, so why do you bother?"

Hmm. Why did I bother? Who was I trying to impress? Nobody! I realized in that moment that makeup is **fun**. I feel more alive than Céline Dion in her *A New Day Has Come* album when my highlighter and concealer are snatched. I could pee myself over a great matte lipstick shade and feel genuinely awake and revived once my foundation is blended. I LOVE makeup! But I love makeup for myself and not anyone else. I love the hobby of painting my face with different shades

of blush, contour makeup, and lipstick. I love all the options. It's just like sewing or crafting, except the art is on you!

But at the same time, I feel pretty dang okay without makeup too. I can own my own face, acne scars, flaky nose, and all. That's just me! And it came as such a shock to me when Sam told me about his view on makeup, because even though I'd gone barefaced around my close friends and even just the world in general, I didn't do that very often. I thought for some weird reason that if I didn't wear makeup, not only would I not look "good," I also wouldn't look "presentable." How nuts!! I actually thought that as a woman, I had to wear makeup when I went places or else I'd come off as lazy. One time I even apologized to a guy for showing up to a meeting WITHOUT MAKEUP! Insane!!

I mean, it wasn't as if I didn't like my face without makeup on: I just thought it was normal to hide your imperfections. Almost necessary. I had a warped mindset about what should be "expected" of me as a woman. But then, hearing someone that wasn't a super-close friend to me tell me he thought it was weird how I wore makeup every day was totally the opposite of what I thought. And it helped me a lot.

So the next day I figured I'd go without makeup because we were planning to go snorkeling and look for turtles. I couldn't cold-turkey it, so I did just my brows and nothing else, and was so proud of how little time I spent on it, and naturally Sam was taking forever in the shower and couldn't even appreciate how quickly I had gotten ready! We went down to the beach and in the ocean and it felt so natural and good, and ever since then I've gone camping for six days without a stitch of makeup on the whole time and it felt so free. Like my skin was breathing extra deep.

I was even more impressed with myself when I was in Bali with Sam and did a photo shoot with him without any makeup on. Not one bit! I had never ever done that before, because I want to look my best. But it was so hot and I knew everything would melt all over my face—and, more important, I really didn't need it.

So now, every time I FaceTime a boy I like, I don't wear makeup. I don't care about it like I used to. I look like me, and that's what matters. All because of what Sam told me up on his roof. Thanks, Sam—you deserve a real shout-out!

CHAPTER 3

BOYS ... and GIRLS

MY FIRST KISS

'm sure you're all thinking, Eva, you seem like you know everything about boys. I'm sure your first kiss was epic! Okay no. My first kiss was horrible. Think a cross between being lightly slapped across the face with a dead fish and having someone poke your belly button after dipping their finger in mayonnaise. That's how uncomfortable my first kiss was. And the craziest part is that the guy who kissed me turned out to have some pretty interesting roles in my life in the future . . . which you'll find out about soon enough.

I was fourteen. It was the summer before I went into high school, and I guess you can say that's when everything changed with boys—since up until then, every boy I ever liked ran away from me.

TIMELINE OF THE BOYS I LIKED WHO NEVER LIKED/LOVED ME BACK

First grade: *Friend-zoned by the cutest boy in school, who became my best friend. Kissed me in a McDonald's PlayPlace and then decided we were better off being friends because having a romantic relationship was too much for a seven-year-old to handle, much less contemplate.*

Seventh grade: *Had a crush on Gary Volder, a surfer boy, changed my Club Penguin log-in to skatesurflove, and all my passwords to surfergirl13, even though I didn't even surf . . . or skate. I'm not even sure he ever knew my first name.*

Seventh to eighth grade: *Moved on from Gary quickly, after realizing he didn't care to know I existed, and started to crush on Jesse Coco, a tall, long-brown-flippy-haired skater boy. Bought a $25 skateboard from Walmart with wheels that didn't spin, and attempted to skate around my apartment complex every day to impress him . . . even though, since the board was so cheap, it couldn't actually go that far easily. I gave up on skateboarding and decided vying for his attention was much easier. Tried to get him to hug me for two years, and when he finally hugged me at school, I got a "misconduct" violation for public affec-*

tion. Yes, you could get in trouble at my school . . . for hugs! I asked him to be my boyfriend and he responded by saying he couldn't because he "already had a girlfriend, who was a high school girl" and showed me a picture of her that he had in his wallet. Funny story is that five years later, after high school graduation, I became friends with the girl in his wallet and she told me she never dated him . . . so that's awkward . . . !

Eighth grade: *Had a crush on Justin, another boy with floppy brown hair. That Lindsay Lohan movie Herbie: Fully Loaded made me fall in love with Justin Long, and Justin looked and acted vaguely similar to Herbie: Fully Loaded's Justin Long, so I'm pretty sure that's why I liked him. He liked to wear a shirt with a ketchup bottle on it. We had staring contests from across the room every day in English class, but when I finally asked him to be my boyfriend on Valentine's Day, he said no.*

Well, I was feeling pretty unlucky when it came to boys, and then I met Ricky. Ricky was an older boy. A junior in high school who had just moved to my apartment complex with his little sister. Now, I've always grown up with a strong attraction to blond-haired, blue-eyed beach boys—I was raised in Orange County, in Southern California, right near the beach, so there was never a shortage of this type, luckily!—and Ricky was as far from that model as possible. However, Ricky had a closet full of Aeropostale hoodies, told me he was on the varsity baseball team, and reeked of the newest line of Hollister cologne, so he interested me.

At the time, my little sister Maya was freaking obsessed with the pool in our apartment complex. Like to the point where our pool would open at 7 a.m., and she'd make me take her bright and early in the morning to swim, and then make me stay until 10 p.m. to watch her, since anyone under the age of fourteen had to be accompanied by someone older. Well, as it turned out, Ricky's little sister loved the pool as well. And so Ricky and I found ourselves spending a lot of time together as we barely kept an eye on our siblings. For a week straight, Ricky and I sat at the pool, talking about boring things, while we watched our little siblings make friends. I didn't even like him. He was uninteresting, unmotivated, and talked to me as if he thought he was a Greek god. But still, he was the only person close to my age at the pool, so I put up with him.

After this week of small-talking chitchat with Ricky at the pool went by, suddenly it was the Fourth of July. Our apartment complex threw a pool party, and of course my sister had to be there. Well, I arrived around sunset, and, as I expected, Ricky was already there. Making friends with my parents!

I slipped into the Jacuzzi because I get cold easily and pools after sunset aren't exactly my favorite temperature, and plus, the Jacuzzi was empty, so I figured it would be a great opportunity to be alone. I leaned back in the bubbling hot water and closed my eyes, enjoying a few blissful moments of relaxing calm.

BAM! I was splashed with water and opened my frustrated eyes to see Ricky getting comfortable alongside of me, with seemingly half the water in the Jacuzzi being spilled everywhere but where it should be. He was really bugging me. Hey dude, I wanted to tell him, I'm just trying to have a moment with myself. Can you please talk about basketball and Hollister somewhere else?

Now, at least at some point in your life, you're going to have a kiss that takes about three million weird and awkward light-years to build up and finally happen. Seriously, I've completed the entire *Lord of the Rings* saga in shorter time than it takes for some boys to kiss me. And in all kiss situations, you're going to feel this weird feeling of magnetization and know that you either want to kiss this person, or know you definitely do NOT want to kiss this person.

So there was Jacuzzi-splashing Ricky, talking to me about the moon and the stars and spouting some other bland one-liners to get me in the mood, and I could feel him scooting closer and closer to me. At this point in my life, I was a freshly born little tadpole. I was instantly confused. I was lost. I was nervous. I didn't know how to wiggle myself out of an awkward situation yet. Suddenly, the fuzzy-magnet feeling inside of me was building to a record-high feeling and all of a sudden . . . *What the f is going on!*—am I being kissed? Ricky was literally windmilling his tongue all over my face. I could barely open my mouth. Was this *kissing*???? WHAT KIND OF SICK PEOPLE DO THIS? I looked to my right, and my PARENTS WERE STILL AT THE POOL, LIKE TWENTY FEET AWAY FROM ME. This was a completely public setting, and I felt like I was being eaten alive. Like, literally, *chill*, Ricky—I ain't the last bit of brownie mix in the bowl after you scooped all you can get into the pan. I was a damn human. Please, don't eat me.

I pushed Ricky off of me out of sheer embarrassment. I literally peaced-out so quick back into my family's humble one-bedroom apartment. I hid there for the next three days, and my sister was mad at me because she no longer had a pool babysitter.

When I finally came around to walking outside at our apartment complex, I ran into some neighborhood kids. They told me that Ricky had been going around saying that I was a bad kisser.

WTF RICKY!

I always think back to this moment and remember my first thought (maybe I would have been an amazing kisser. I wouldn't know since I WASNT EVEN ABLE TO OPEN MY MOUTH!). I think the bad kisser was Ricky, because everyone since him has told me I'm an amazing kisser . . . but that's beside the point. *Sips the tea!*

I managed to dodge the Ricky bullet for the rest of the summer until I eventually had to run into him in high school. I was way wrong about Ricky's "cool guy" persona. He actually ended up being a huge pain in the ass who pretty much no one liked. And he was never on varsity baseball. Ricky apparently wasn't over the fact that I didn't fall in love with him after his fish kiss, and he decided he still wasn't done being a part of my life yet, either . . .

Remember Justin? The sweet brown-haired boy in the ketchup shirt who I wanted so badly in junior high? Well, shortly into the first few weeks of high school, Justin and I were going strong as just friends. I wasn't into him anymore, as summer had come and gone and there were too many cute blond high school boys to meet from different junior highs.

Because Justin didn't like me as a girlfriend, I stopped thinking of him as a potential boyfriend. I just didn't like him like that anymore—and I was actually so proud of myself for getting over it! Justin became a pretty close member of my best friend group, and we were able to be friends and hang out in a group and everything, with zero expectations that anything was ever going to change between us.

Well, over the summer I had that pretty messy and unwanted first kiss with Ricky that I didn't like very much, and honestly I didn't even get to kiss him back, so I was still pretty hyped on getting my first REAL kiss that I got to participate in.

One week after high school had started, Justin came up to me in the hallway and said, "Hey, Eva, I left my sweater in science class. Do you want to come and get it with me after school?"

I said sure, of course. Cool. We were friends. I didn't like going into empty classrooms on my own either. No biggie.

So I agreed to go with Justin to fetch his sweater, and we met up after school, walked across a nearly empty campus, and headed around to the back way of the new building, where Mrs. Michael's earth science class was.

By the time we got to the room, I was starting to feel pretty weirded out, since we completely bypassed the easy way to get to the building and went the back, secret-staircase way that no one ever used. We got to the door and I tried to open it. It was locked. Of course it was! It was like 3:10 and the school day ended at 2:40! I turned around and all of a sudden I saw Justin throwing me the most half-nervous, half-ready-for-action face I'd ever seen.

Oh no. *Le sigh.*

"Um, Justin," I said, putting my hand on the doorknob and trying it again. Yep. It was locked. "We can't even get in to get your sweater."

"I know," he said. "So, like, what's up?"

I looked at him, bewildered. "What?" I asked. "What are you talking about, what's up?

He smiled, but then he looked away and I realized he was really nervous or something. "Eva," he replied, "I really like you."

"What?" I said again, as he still wouldn't meet my eyes. "I thought you didn't like me, Justin. You made that perfectly clear last year."

"I was wrong," he said, "I do like you. I really like you a lot."

"Oh," I said, "okay. Whatever."

I was still kind of skeptical when he

finally looked at me again, and then he started walking toward me. I started walking backward and felt my back lean up against the staircase railing. I was WTFing so hard right then.

"Just hug me," Justin said.

Justin continued walking toward me, with his arms out. I can't resist a good hug. So of course I hugged my friend Justin. And then, out of nowhere, he KISSED ME. I mean, *really* kissed me. A kiss that was kind of weirdly innocent because it was the last thing I was expecting, and really kind of smooth and sexy at the same time. It wasn't a full-on make-out session, but it wasn't a peck, either! So we start kissing. The whole time in my mind I was like WTF, I don't like Justin anymore, now Justin likes ME??!?!? I DONT HAVE TIME FOR THESE GAMES. But on the other hand, I sure did like being kissed . . . soooo . . . I'ma just ride this one out.

And then all of a sudden I heard a bunch of people around me. My ears tuned in. It was high-pitched girly snickering and giggling. Seemed like none other than . . . .

THE ENTIRE VARSITY CHEER TEAM.

I turned around and saw the entire varsity cheer team, in their cheer outfits, staring at us and laughing. They'd been taking this same path to go to their practice after school, and literally busted

Justin and me having our weirdly innocent but definitely scandalous kiss.

I knew a lot of the girls on the team because I'd grown up with them and we'd gone to junior high together. So they knew it was me . . . Eva. They also knew Justin because Justin was honestly pretty popular with everyone in school . . . So there I was, me, Eva, busted making out with Justin. Well, this was awkward.

I could tell from Justin's face that he'd had no idea they were about to show up, but he seemed way less embarrassed by this predicament than I was.

I was so mortified that I just picked up my backpack and ran.

My parents picked me up and I sat in the backseat, staring mindlessly out the window, thinking about what had happened all the way home. Why had Justin kissed me like that? If he liked me, after all, why hadn't he said something sooner? What was *really* going on?

Justin didn't call me or text me that night. At school the next day everything went back to 110 percent normal. We never even discussed it. It was like it never happened. Justin was part of my friend group—and so everything continued normally. We'd just hang out, with the rest of our friends, and neither of us said anything about that infamously random-AF kiss.

Then things got even weirder. I

hadn't really thought that much about Justin because, I realized, I only liked him as a friend and I didn't want to be his girlfriend. We only had one class together, and he was in band and re-hearsed a lot so I hardly saw him outside of lunch period. So when he asked me to grab his guitar in the band room about two weeks later, I said sure. It was a per-fectly understandable request. He was my good platonic friend and I figured we'd just scoop up his guitar and head to lunch with the rest of the gang.

Instead, there was no guitar to pick up. And he tried to kiss me AGAIN.

"Honestly, WTF, Justin," I said. "I don't like you like that. We're not going to go out or anything. What is going on?"

"Oh, come on, Eva," he said, looking at me with a dopey, romantic smile.

"Sorry I'm so confused," I replied, a little pissed off. "My crush on you was in junior high. You know that."

"Yeah, I know," he said, but he didn't seem upset in the slightest.

"Just one kiss," he said. So I planted a quick, awkward, and slightly annoyed one on him and scurried off to lunch with-out him, where he met up with the group shortly after. We didn't say a word about what happened.

What was going on?

I had no idea. Because it went on for years!

Every few weeks or so, Justin would try to kiss me. The first time, okay, I did kiss him back a little and he was honestly pretty good as kissing went, but then I realized I still didn't like him as anything but just friends. I was actually already on to someone new: Ben.

But Justin kept on trying. Sometimes he'd sort of pounce on me in the hallway and give me a kiss before I could react. Or one time we went to tryouts for the talent show together, and he started play-ing his guitar for me and trying to kiss me on the grass at night. By sophomore year I told him it had to stop. It did, for a while, especially when he saw me dating other people, and things went on as normal—we were in the same group hanging out after school and nobody ever knew that any of this had happened. He didn't bring it up and I sure wasn't going to. Literally none of our friends ever knew, and a lot of them still don't know!

Fast-forward to my senior year. It was toga day, where we all got to dress up in sheets and wear lace-up sandals and pretend we were ancient Greeks and basically look ridiculous. So, that day— I'd basically pushed Justin and his crazy kissing out of my memory bank, as by that point it had been over a year since he'd tried anything—when Justin asked me to help him clean up the lunch area after the period was up, I said sure. I never needed an excuse to be a little bit late for math class!

It didn't take very long to do the cleanup and then we walked to his algebra class, and just as we got to the door where I was going to drop him off, boom, he pulled me close and tried to kiss me again. This time, I got really mad as I pushed him away.

"What the hell, Justin," I told him. "Why do you keep trying to kiss me? IT'S LITERALLY SENIOR YEAR AND I'VE HAD ENOUGH."

He shrugged. "Oh, just kiss me once. It's no big deal."

"Well, it is to me," I replied, now even angrier.

"Whatever," he said, and went into his classroom and shut the door.

Later that day, I was still steaming about it, so I talked to another girl I knew who also was friends with Justin. Guess what? He had been pulling the same stunt with her! I never did figure out what was going on with that situation, and it wasn't until a year after high school that I told some of my close friends about this because—you got it—Justin kept on trying to kiss me when we were in college! We would go to parties at our best friend's house, and if Justin found me alone in the kitchen getting a drink, he'd try to pounce on me.

The craziest thing was that I could

never be *too* mad at Justin. Now, this being said, what he had done, friend or not, was unwelcome. I played it off, but a different girl could have handled it much more seriously. Regardless, if I had been stronger and wiser, like I am now, I would have stopped him dead in his tracks and said NO. What he was doing was inappropriate and done. But I was only a teenager and wasn't strong enough to be that harsh to a guy.

Now I know better. If someone is making you feel uncomfortable, you need to let them know that's not how to treat someone, or find someone to help you let him know.

Part of the problem too was that Justin had been in the squad since the very beginning. He was a true friend to me for longer than some of my girlfriends stayed around, and still to this day is someone I play video games with on the couch, drive late at night to get cheap drive-through Mexican food with, and give relationship advice to. He was the OG homie, and a few dozen innocent kiss attempts weren't enough for me to stay mad at him. I mean, after all, I love to kiss too. I can't argue with that.

Well, one day in college, I just couldn't take it anymore, and I confronted him at a party we were both at and demanded to know the truth. "Remember freshman year, when you kissed me and all the cheerleaders saw?" I asked him. "Why did you do that? Did you really like me?"

Justin got a funny look on his face. "Yeah, I liked you," he admitted. "But not *like* like. I kissed you because I got dared to."

My jaw practically dropped to the floor. "You got dared to? Like, what the hell?"

"Sorry, Eva," he said, but he didn't look sorry one little bit.

"You mean you got dared every single time you tried to kiss me?"

"No. Just that first time. My friends knew you'd liked me in junior high, and they were like let's pick on Eva and see if she'll kiss you back if you try. So I did."

I was low-key embarrassed, but it had been so long ago that It was honestly kind of funny at this point. I still couldn't get mad at him. Well, okay, I was mad for a few seconds. But we were good friends, and had been through so many amazing times despite the weird secret kissing parts. I just saw the kissing as just one of his stupid boy moments.

So that's the story of Justin and the thousand kisses.

 Blond boys always get the best of me. I learned that with Ben. Ben made me end up in a neck brace . . . but I'll explain that later.

I met Ben in Spanish class freshman year, and I instantly fell in love. There he was, just my type. He was tall and skinny. He had that dirty blond hair that was styled with the little floppy top part that every boy seems to go through at some point. He wore canvas-colored pants with a striped gray tee, and he had a sporty, no-nonsense blue backpack that held his dirty cross-country shoes poking out at the top. He wore black-framed glasses. He was nerdy and adorable, and resembled a young Michael Cera circa *Juno*.

Days passed and I didn't say much to Ben. He sat in front of me, and would always have his little first-generation iPod blasting an eclectic mix of music that I'd never heard before, but instantly loved.

I still remember the first time I made my move on Ben. I asked him what he was listening to, and he said Nickasaur. (You can look it up—it's pretty terrible music.) However, back then Nickasaur was the shit, and I said I loved it too and he smiled.

Ben and I became musical twins. He would show me all this amazing music (which I promise sounded ten times better than Nickasaur). And our love of both some terrible and some amazing music led to us hanging out in between classes, and then hanging out at lunch, and then finally hanging out at the local movie theater.

I was thrilled when he asked me out to the movies. My first real date! No chaperone! Grandma would stay home and I could go out with a boy I liked! I got to the movie theater around 2 p.m., and we watched *Cloudy with a Chance of Meatballs*, and then went to Starbucks afterward to buy our very first coffee drink (so adult!), which was a new drink Starbucks was trying out called the London Fog. It tasted like warm Froot Loops, and we bonded over that hard.

Somehow, I got lucky enough to call Ben my first boyfriend that I ever had. Amazingly, he lived right across the street from me, so we did everything together and hung out all the time, always at his house, where his mom would feed us frozen grapes and this interesting cranberry salad that I scarfed down even though it always upset my stomach. We had Halloween together, Christmas together, New Year's Eve together, and more. He had this attic upstairs that was turned into a family room with a TV and beanbags and all, so that's where we spent most of our days. We talked. We walked hand in hand. We hugged. We kissed occasionally, and I remember the only time we ever made out was on New Year's night, on the couch in that family room . . . which was super weird and we stopped after a solid ten seconds.

It was just a really nice, really inno-cent, really great friendship. Me and Ben. Who was a shrimpy sort of white kid with shaggy blond hair with a nerdy sort of messenger bag. He was on the track team. He was really smart. Soft-spoken, just a really nice guy. That's who Ben was.

I was crazy head-over-heels in love with him! And then, all of a sudden, he just broke up with me.

That's it. Nothing was wrong. I was SO confused.

Left heartbroken, I cried day and night over losing the one person I called closer than a boyfriend, and closer than a best friend. Like I said, I called him my twin! He was my second half, and he ended our relationship with no real expla-nation, except for the tired old cliché "It's not you, it's me." Literally. He said that.

Freshman boy quotes, people.

Months went by of me literally bawl-ing my stomach and all my organs out over Ben, who seemed to have moved on perfectly fine, until somehow, the next year on, we started dating again.

But before that happened, fast-forward to me as a sophomore, and Ben and I were in the same drama class. One day, a new girl named Maddie moved in from Corona. She was beautiful. She had boobs that looked like they belonged on a freaking twenty-eight-year-old fitness model. Her hair was golden shiny blond. She had the biggest blue-green eyes I'd ever seen, and freckles all over her nose and cheeks, which I would have died to have had. And, of course, she showed up, the new girl in school, wearing a baby-blue cotton midi-dress with a sweetheart neckline, sandal heels (who tf wears those in high school?), and reading A BOOK. A BOOK, PEOPLE. LIKE, COME ON.

She strolled into my drama class, and Ben was staring at her the way everyone else in the classroom was staring at her, and then he came over to me and whispered the words "She's cute." She's *cute*???!!?!? WHAT WAS HE TRYING TO DO TO ME, KILL ME??? She's *cute*?! The f?!

My heart got warm and heavy. I felt a mango tree growing in my chest. WTF.

The next class we had was English, and I went to my seat—oh freaking perfect—as Maddie then walked in and sat herself down on the seat next to me. She opened her book—which, by the way, had no freaking book cover, so it literally just looked like an old, perfect, out-of-a-1600s-movie book. I turned to look at her she went, "Hi! I'm Maddie!" At this point I was trying to hide the furiousness that was on the back of my tongue. "Hi. I'm Eva," I said, willing my voice to be calm. "My ex-boyfriend thinks you're cute!" My eye twitched a little bit more and I turned back in my seat. I was flipping out inside.

Well, it turned out that Ben didn't actually like Maddie, after all, and Maddie started working with me on a group project a week later in drama class, where we ended up becoming best friends for almost seven years! But that's another story.

Ben and I got back together a few months later, until a legitimate reason to break up happened. At this time, a lot of my friends that I met freshman year, who'd sworn off drugs and alcohol with me, started doing drugs anyway. At first it started with weed, but it quickly moved to other, more intense things. Luckily, I was never around when they did them, so I just got to hear the crazy stories at school of what had happened the night before, instead. Ben was being pressured into trying these drugs with the group, and even though I tried my absolute hardest to talk him out of it all, I couldn't, and it ended up with a giant fight at the same movie theater where we'd had our first date, when I told him I couldn't date him if he started doing drugs. His argument was that he only wanted to try weed once, just to know what it was like, and then he'd stop—but we both knew that was a sorry excuse. I told him that if he started smoking weed with this group of people, he might continue down a bad road. He got mad at me, and I ran off crying.

We didn't talk to each other for the rest of the school year. Until I made probably one of the most embarrassing mistakes of my life, and wrote Ben a two-page, back-and-front LITERAL love letter on some spare notebook paper. In the note, I wrote everything. Everything from how I missed his mom's frozen grapes to how I missed his dog. How I was still thinking about him day and night. How I realized . . . that I was in love with him.

I tried my hardest to origami-fold it up, even though I had no idea how to make anything other than a cootie catcher, and when I was staying at my grandma's house I had her drive me to Ben's street so I could drop it off. It had taken me two days to write perfectly, and I had drawn hearts all over it once it was done. This love letter was my last resort. I knew Ben was taking a weeklong trip to Hawaii with his family over spring break, and so I figured he'd have all spring break to figure out how he would tell me that he loved me back. I handed him the note confidently and hopped back into my grandma's serial killer van. We drove off, and the waiting began.

Except Ben never got back to me. Days went by and then a week, and then I came to a horrible realization. What the hell had I done??? I DIDN'T LOVE BEN LIKE THAT. At least not anymore! Ben was my friend. Ben meant the world to

me. And in that moment, I leveled up in maturity hard. I was only fifteen, but I realized I knew one thing for sure: Did I love Ben? Yes. I loved him with half of my heart and soul. But loving someone and being IN love with someone are completely different things. I loved Ben. I loved my best friends. I loved my family. I would do anything for them and would die to see them upset or sad. I cared for them. That's the type of love I felt for Ben.

And then I realized that you reach a point after a breakup (if you and your ex stay cool) where you have nothing but love and care for this person, even if you aren't together anymore and you've moved on. You still wish them the best and want to see them succeed and be happy. That's what I felt for Ben! I didn't need to date him anymore. I had cured my own lovesickness. I just simply wanted him to know I cared about him.

Except the damage was done. Ben had the letter, and he now thought I was a creepy stalker girl. Ben got back to me finally a week later and told me he just wanted to be friends. I couldn't have agreed more . . . though after that note was sent I'm sure he didn't believe a word I said to him. The year ended with Ben and me kind of avoiding each other out of embarrassment on my part.

Junior year came and Ben and I

still weren't talking much, until one day, something horrible happened. I still remember this so clearly. I was out with my friends and saw on the called ID that it was Ben. I got extremely excited. Did he like me again? Did he need the homework for a class? Did he want to tell me about the new tomato tree his brother had planted? (I kept up with his family on Facebook a little too closely . . .) But when I answered the phone, it wasn't Ben who was on the line—it was his mom, and she sounded really scared. She told me that Ben was in the hospital. He had been skateboarding near his grandma's house during a visit and decided to go down a giant hill, where he ended up not being able to turn his board enough. He went straight into oncoming traffic, fell off his board, and landed in a bush across the intersection. His skull was cracked open, and he was in a really bad state. His mom told me that Ben asked her to call me.

OMG what? I hadn't spoken to Ben in like forever. Suddenly I felt a huge responsibility to be there for him. He meant so much to me, fights or embarrassment or not. I stayed in touch with his mom while Ben was in the hospital, and after a few days, he was finally released. An hour later, I rode my bike across the street to his house to see him.

Ben looked better than I thought he would, and we watched *Ponyo*, a Japanese anime film, and ate his mom's familiar frozen grapes. All the good times we'd had together flooded back into my mind. And then, halfway through the movie, he paused it and looked at me. I asked him to explain what exactly had happened with his accident. Ben sighed and told me all about how he was being reckless and went down the giant hill and hit his head. Part of me thought maybe he hit his head on the hill, or maybe he even hurt himself while on drugs but he just didn't want to tell me. Then he went on, adding how once he got out of the hospital, he realized that God had given him another chance at life and that he was being stupid falling into drugs and bad people and peer pressure. He was speaking so much from the heart that I literally started to cry for him. This was Ben. My Ben. My friend. The Ben I grew up with and shared so many memories with . . . and here he was, sharing something so deep with me.

I was so happy for him realizing a big part of himself, and in that moment, Ben and I were cool again. I still had some feelings for him—mostly because he was an amazing guy and I was jealous of whoever got to call him theirs in the future, especially because I knew it wouldn't be me. But I was no longer mad at Ben or weird with him. We were okay.

Once he was fully recovered, Ben

completely switched his life around. Like complete 180. Suddenly he was getting straight A's and in all honors classes, and he started senior year off with a totally revamped style. He had a canvas messenger bag with indie band pins all over it, brand-new glasses, and a cool hipster swag to him. Ben convinced me to join yearbook, and I was excited not only because I'd get to really express myself creatively . . . but because I'd be close to him again.

It was in yearbook that I realized Ben had become a total ladies' man, and nearly all the girls in class were obsessed with him. I could easily see why. I mean, Ben had everything a girl wanted. He was clean, well-dressed, smart, loved to read, and could even bake. He got really close to a girl named Leah in class, and together they started a cupcake company, where they'd hand-bake well-decorated cupcakes for people at school. Ben would often bake his favorite gluten-free poppy-seed mini-cupcakes and bring them for the yearbook class. He had a yellow Lab named Tracy and loved to take photos of her. Ben was goals. AF.

I went about all senior year jealous of Leah and Ben. Leah was Ben's new me, and they did everything together. Everything I used to do with him and more. They would make matching Halloween costumes, like Juno and Paulie Bleeker,

and for senior dress-up days, they would wear couples costumes.

Everyone in the entire school who knew Ben and Leah would joke about them getting married. Even I deep down felt like it was a total possibility. And Leah and I weren't super close friends, but every time she'd look at me I'd get that feeling in her mind that she knew who I was and what I'd had, and now *she* was the one who had him. I was jealous of her, but more so happy for her and him.

Nonetheless, by the end of senior year, Ben had still not asked Leah to be his girlfriend, which the entire school thought was really odd. So I decided to be a good friend to Leah and see if I could convince Ben to ask her out, since I knew she absolutely adored him.

During our senior yearbook trip up to the mountains, I was alone with Ben in the cabins one night, which made me feel really cool and adult, being alone in a cabin with a boy I liked . . . BUT FOCUS, EVA. THIS ISN'T ABOUT YOU. IT'S ABOUT BEN AND LEAH'S OBVIOUS LOVE.

I sat on the couch next to Ben and just came out with it. "Ben, do you like Leah?" I asked. STRAIGHT SAVAGE MODE.

To my surprise, he laughed out loud and said, "LEAH? I could never date someone with the same name as my mom!" Damn. You're right. Ben's mom's name WAS Leah . . .

But I wasn't going to give up. I knew Leah liked him, and I felt like he could just be lying to protect my feelings, so I pressed on.

"Ben," I said, "Leah told me she's never been asked on a date. Why won't you just ask her to the movies and take her on one?"

Ben looked away for a sec and then responded with a coy, "Eva, I don't *like* Leah." I blinked. Wait, WTF? He then proceeded to go off on a random tangent. "My mom really misses you. You need to come over again. We know each other so well, Eva. You know who I like. You'll find out soon enough."

OKAY. WHAT THE HELL. SORRY.

In this moment, my heart turned into fried dumplings. I immediately ran to my girlfriends and gave them this hot boiling tea.

"YOU KNOW WHO I LIKE. YOU'LL FIND OUT SOON ENOUGH???"

These words haunted me for the next few days, weeks, months.

Did Ben like . . . *me*??? Was that what he was trying to say? I WAS SO CON-FUSED.

Well, as time went by, Ben was put on the back burner, since I was already kind of dating someone else, and plus, Ben was so 2009 and this was 2012. I couldn't

be dwelling on the past. It was senior year, and I was in another relationship. But then my love of dance came along and decided to scramble all of my emotions up one final time.

At the time, Adele's "Someone Like You" was the hippest song on the radio and all the rage in the dance world. Girls were choreographing mediocre lyrical solos to it left and right. And one day I came into dance class to find out that we were taking a lyrical combo class with a guest teacher.

Suddenly I was being motivationally screamed at, like most dance teachers always seemed to do, to "DIG DEEP INTO YOUR SOUL. FIND WHO THIS DANCE IS ABOUT. FEEL THIS SONG. FEEL IT!" I was tossing, turning, flipping, and throwing my body to the floor all while being coached to feel the music. The room was spinning, and every time the guest dance teacher replayed the song and shouted out, "FEEL THOSE LYRICS, LISTEN TO THOSE LYRICS, LADIES," I kept thinking of Ben. You know, those famous lyrics:

I heard that your dreams came true
Guess she gave you things I didn't give to you

TOTALLY ABOUT LEAH, RIGHT!!!!

HELLO, ADELE. THANK YOU SO MUCH FOR SINGING THESE LYRICS THAT MADE ME FEEL LIKE I'M NOT CRAZY FOR STILL GOING AFTER BEN.

And then, Adele started belting out the lyrics "NEVER MIND, I'LL FIND SOMEONE LIKE YOOOOOOOOOOUUUUUU . . ."

That's when things went downhill. My dance team split up into small groups and the rest of the sixteen girls went and sat down while I stayed standing in front of them, with two other dancers at my side. The song started up again and I began to dance, doing exactly what the guest teacher had told us to do:

FEEL THE LYRICS.

I got really emotional. *Way* too emotional. As in crying hysterically emo. Which is not good when you're trying to focus on dancing and doing the moves correctly. I went in to do my perfect triple pirouette into a floor slide, and my emotional energy took control of me. I slipped on what could only have been some of my wet tears of the floor, and I fell awkwardly down, landing ON MY NECK. I WAS TEMPORARILY PARALYZED. I COULD NOT MOVE THE UPPER HALF OF MY BODY.

Suddenly the room was spinning and there was a lot of yelling and I was so terrified I couldn't even speak. I couldn't move. I literally could not move my neck!

The rest of what happened was a blur but I was taken to the emergency room and they did all these X-rays and I walked out wearing a neck brace. I was incredibly lucky the damage wasn't catastrophic. Can you imagine if I'd seriously paralyzed myself while dancing to Adele because I was crying over a boy who didn't love me back? That would have been the most pathetic thing ever.

I was so embarrassed that I didn't go to classes for a solid week because I didn't want anyone to see me. No way was I up to explaining that I fell because my ex-boyfriend wrecked my emotions so badly to the point of me being temporarily paralyzed.

And I didn't want to see Ben either, and I knew I would, because he was in my drama class.

So when I finally had to go to school to pick up my assignments, I tied an enormous scarf around the brace in a pretty pathetic attempt at hiding it. The scarf, though, was from the dollar store, and was made of this super-cheap thin fabric, so everyone could clearly see the neck brace underneath it. Luckily, I barely escaped Ben, and to this day he still doesn't know I was so emotional about him in dance class that I could have ended up in a wheelchair!

Ben and I ended up going to the same college, and two years in, I still never had proper closure of what exactly had been going on with the two of us all throughout high school. He became close friends with a friend I met in college, and I got to run into him as distant friends a lot around campus, and that's when I saw the same game happen.

Ben had made a new best girlfriend named Mandy, and she was in love with him. But Ben had no interest in dating her, and our entire friend group had no idea why. I mean, Mandy was hot. She was a dancer with beautiful brown hair, and her Facebook profile photo was of her doing a leap on the beach.

Months and months of college went by, and finally I asked my friend Caroline what was going on with Ben and Mandy. I mean, come ON, Ben, you can't possibly miss out on Leah AND hot Mandy. Caroline looked at me with wide eyes of shock, and then she said, "Eva, Ben's gay."

Ben was gay.
Oh.
The whole time.
And I was the only girlfriend he'd ever have.

Shortly after she told me this, I finally got to talk to Ben on my own and catch up on the literal six years of closure I never got. Turns out, Ben had been gay since—and I quote—he "popped out of his mom's womb." He told me that he never had the courage to come out in high school, and even though he loved me like his best friend, he didn't exactly know how to tell me, "Hey, instead of dating me . . . want me to be your gay best friend?" It made so much sense. All the unexplained breakups. The girls he was always with that took my place. The perfectly frosted cupcakes . . . tooooo perfectly frosted. The way he told me that I knew who he liked! Duh! He liked BOYS.

When I was in high school, I'm sorry to have to say, admitting you were gay was just not a thing, especially in my community. No one was "out," except for a few lesbian girls that I low-key thought about kissing a few times. Ben being gay never once entered my head when he started breaking up with me. There was never any explanation of why, so I kept thinking it was me; that I'd done something wrong or was a terrible, unlovable person. There were no excuses like the ones my friends were hearing when they got the "talk." You know, the excuses like, "Oh, sorry. I cheated on you." "Oh, I like someone else." "Oh, you're not good enough."

Not Ben. All he'd say was, "Eva, it's not you—it's me. You'll find out soon enough."

But I didn't.

And now I finally did find out. Six years later.

I was so happy for Ben for finding himself and that I had been such a huge part of him growing up. I got to be there for him and see his journey, and he turned out so, so incredibly happy, and he still is today.

What I learned from this is #1, when you're going to go through the most insanely dramatic breakup ever, it is going to hurt and you're not going to exactly know how to cope with this because let's be honest, in high school I didn't even know what lunch was going to be the next day, and I sure as hell didn't know how to handle the serious breakup of a relationship that was really important to me.

You're going to cry for hours, days, weeks, and, in my case, years. And that's okay, because as long as, through it all, you know that there's a light at the end of the tunnel, you'll take as much time as you need before you're ready to find that tunnel light, hunny. Even though high school continued on and our relationship most definitely was over, Ben was still on my mind for years afterward, like any first love rightfully would be. And to be completely honest, had Ben not turned out to be gay, he would probably still be on my mind, driving me crazy. He, like anyone else you'll ever date, will always come with a big "What if?" What if Ben and I had worked out? What if we had gotten married and had a house in the suburbs and three children and two dogs and a couple of gerbils together? What if he had married someone hotter than me and more successful and he became even happier and more successful and more settled in life before I did, and I ended up living with fifty cats and a bucketful of remorse? I can't lie and tell you all these thoughts won't swirl in your head, drive you crazy, and even make you cry sometimes. Even years after the breakup.

It's a little thing called nostalgia, which is one of my favorite words. It's what you feel when you can't help but look back and reminisce on all the good old times, and with Ben, as well as a lot of other boys, friends, and moments in life, I am nostalgic.

It's okay to be nostalgic. It's on those Tumblr "cool word" pages for a reason. It's a feeling everyone has and is okay to have, and it's not a bad feeling!

Memories are beautiful, and wanting to go back to the good old days of eating the frozen grapes his mother made with Ben while taking a walk down our old neighborhood street is totally normal.

But it took me a while to find nostalgia in the memory, and not regret.

Having a relationship end, whether friendship, romantic, or anything else, isn't something to regret.

Now whenever I give someone advice—someone who is going through their first "real" breakup and literally cannot function—I just tell them, "Look, I'm not going to lie. That was 110 percent me." I cried so much I thought I gave myself the flu most nights. You know that nasty cry when you realize like ten minutes into it that you also can't breathe out of your nose and suddenly you have a headache and your eyes are all puffy and your cheeks are salty with tears? That's the type of cry that's only reserved for really intense sad stuff . . . and your first real breakup.

Everything after this becomes a hell of a lot easier. You realize after taking way too much time crying over your first love that, hey, it was only my first love, and it sure as hell won't be my last love, so now that that's over . . . okay, fine, let's get on our feet and move on.

If Ben had been my last love, I don't even know who I would be right now or what type of life I'd be living. A completely different one, that's for sure. Dating is about learning things. Dating is about enjoying life and time with someone. Dating isn't meant to work out perfectly every single time. In fact, it's not meant to work out MOST of the time. But that's the whole point—it's what makes dating so much fun! And trust me, as you get older you start to realize dating *is* so much fun.

I also learned #2: Not everyone is who they say they are, and not everyone's actions reflect who they really are on the inside. High school is not always going to be a place where people feel comfortable being themselves. In all honesty, most people in high school will be too scared to show who they really are on the inside, because they're scared of being judged. Everyone has a deeper meaning to what they're doing. Bullies aren't just bullies because they like being mean. Bullies are bullies because they're channeling their own problems into anger toward other people. Haters don't like to hate for fun. They're hating because they aren't comfortable with who they are, and want to tear others down for *them* being comfortable.

You'll find out as you get older, and the pressure to put on this fake show in high school goes away, that every-one is going through *something*, and you should never take the way some-one else is treating you as a reflection of something *you're* doing wrong. It isn't you at all. You're just caught in the crossfire of someone else figuring themselves out, and that's going to happen a lot, and that's okay. Every time Ben broke up with me, or told me that he didn't like me back enough to be my boyfriend, I stayed awake for hours and days wondering why. What had I done? What had I said? What had I meant? Like, I knew deep down that I hadn't done a single thing wrong . . . so it must have meant my personality wasn't good enough, or there was someone better than me, or I wasn't pretty enough or smart enough for him. But of course it was none of those things. It wasn't my fault. Ben's issues had nothing to do with me. At the time, though, I thought it was only my fault, and that tore me apart.

Don't let anyone else's journey influ-ence the way you reflect on your own. Let your life play out and keep moving at a forward pace. Don't put your life on halt for a boy, and remember that, eventually, every story in your life will come full circle . . . even if it takes seven years. :)

I was always into romance and boys and all of that fun stuff. Even when I was very, very little. Do you remember the preschool boy I was friend-zoned by? Well, his name was Liam. It didn't take long for me to lock my interests on Liam. I remember it clearly. My mom had just dropped me off at the Catholic preschool right down the street from my grandma's house. It was a humble single-story setup built on a 2,000-square-foot plot of dead grass. Right in the middle of the school was a rusty green gate that would open in the morning to let all of the kids in. Right as my mom had left me in the hands of what was to be my first teacher ever, the rusty gate slid open and unveiled the most epic playground my eyes had ever feasted on. TWO yellow slides, one straight and one curvy. I'd seen those before and was unimpressed, so my eyes kept wandering. A pirate lookout! That was new! My eyes kept moving until boom! I landed on the mother of all suburban playground activ-ities: a tire swing. A **giant** tire too! Like a monster truck tire! Big enough for one . . . two . . . maybe three preschool kids to sit on!! I started to run over to the tire swing and noticed a kid sitting, facing away from me. I saw a head full of pin-straight, golden blond hair.

I kept running toward the tire swing until I got close enough for the blond kid to notice my presence, and then I realized the little blond kid was a boy.

Before I knew it, like in some fairy-tale romance, the blond boy hopped off the tire swing and turned around slowly. Everything around him went blurry, for me.

"Hi, I'm Liam!" he said.

Liam was mine.

I was only around five, but I started acting like Scar from *The Lion King*, thinking, The boy is mine. Bring him to me. Alive.

At the time, even at such a young age, I was extremely obsessed with Leonardo DiCaprio from *Titanic*, and when I gazed upon Liam all I could see was him dressed up in a little tux at the top of a staircase, raising a box of apple juice in the air and giving me a smile.

Liam and I became instant best friends, and even though I was only five, I definitely knew I was attracted to him beyond belief. He lived right up the street from me on the top of this giant, steep hill, and every day from the beginning of school to the end of the night, Liam and I would play together at the playground. On birthdays, we would always fight to get each other the best presents, and on his seventh birthday I got him a blow-up *Star Wars* chair, and he got me a white feather boa, which I cherished for years, and even when 90 percent of the feathers

had fallen out, I still kept it. He was my absolute favorite person.

Liam and I were so close as friends: he was the first, genuine best friend I really ever had. I thought we would live happily ever after, but in second grade, things changed. My family decided to move out of my grandparents' house to an apartment in the next city over, and I had to change schools . . . which meant I had to leave Liam. I didn't exactly know what I was getting myself into at the time, and I didn't know that meant I would have to leave Liam forever. I mean, I was in second grade. I had no phone to text him, and no Instagram to stalk him on. I remember the day before the big move, I sat in class and wrote Liam a note on colored construction paper. I told him that I was moving away and I didn't know if we would ever see each other again and I'd miss him so much and that we'd be friends forever. I put a little sticker of Winnie the Pooh on it, and drew a bear holding hands with another bear. My grandma had this weird habit of getting me mini phone-book notebooks to write all my friends' numbers in, but I would always lose them. And so after the big move, I lost Liam's number.

Years went by and I made new friends, and suddenly I was a sophomore in high school and hadn't seen Liam since that fateful day in second grade nearly nine years before! I always thought about him, though. It was crazy, because I knew him back in literal beginning of elementary school and was head over heels for him. I wondered what he could possibly look like as a teenager, and if his hair was still golden blond. I wondered if he still might live close by, like up the street from me as he once did. I wondered if he still had that *Star Wars* blow-up chair. I wondered if he still ever thought about me or remembered me.

And I think the scariest thought I had was, Did I mean as much to him as he meant to me? Occasionally, I'd have to remind myself that I probably would never see him again, and that I needed to let go.

Well, one day I was shopping with my mom in a random Target, MILES away from the city where we were then living and even further from my old city where Liam lived, and I was in the dressing room trying on some snazzy layering tanks when I heard my mom gasp outside the door. Then she said, "Oh my God, no way!" Her conversation was muffled, but I could tell that my mom was chatting it up with what seemed to be another lady outside the door. I could tell from the tone of her voice that she was excited—my mom got LOUD when she was excited. I quickly threw on my own shirt, gathered the tank

tops, and left the room to see a lady that looked vaguely familiar. No way. It couldn't be. Why was she here??? IT WAS LIAM'S MOM.

I thought: This is fate.

I was so happy to see her, because it meant that Liam was still somewhere out there, and at least his mom remembered me, so that was a good sign that maybe he would too. His mom told me they still lived in the same house up the street from my grandma's, and that he went to the high school right by my grandma's house! She added that Liam was out of town on a snowboarding trip with his dad, but to add him on Facebook. The last thing she said was that she was sure Liam would be pleased to hear from me.

I felt like I had a new lease on LIFE. Liam was alive! He had been right up the street all along! All those days I had gone back to my grandma's to visit—and he was only a few hundred feet from me, doing whatever growing boys do.

So I added him on Facebook and started stalking. No girlfriend. His golden blond hair had changed to a dirty blond, and it was long and flippy. He wore hats. He wasn't as cute as I wanted him to still be, but he was all right, and that would have to do. He was on the swim team and oooh . . . had a few shirtless Speedo photos for me to browse. I started getting this weird idea that he would definitely be my boyfriend once we met. Like this was *Finding Dory* and I was Dory just trying to reunite with my family and live happily ever after.

We started messaging each other and I was thrilled that he remembered me! After a few days of messaging, we even Skyped, with my entire family and his reconnecting in a big online reunion. It was decided that in a few days, Liam and I would meet up.

I was ecstatic to see Liam again, but I knew to see him I would have to first get a ride to my grandma's house back in my old neighborhood. I thought my grandparents would be happy about my recent reconnection with Liam, but when I told them that we were back in touch, Papi frowned.

"There's talk," he said, "you know, from the neighbors. No one likes Liam anymore. They don't trust him. They say he's kind of a jerk."

Okay, Papi. First of all, no one calls anyone a jerk anymore. Also, you have to be wrong. Liam is cool and this is going to work out just fine.

That's what I put off to Papi, but even I had to admit from my Facebook stalking that Liam was what Papi Gutowski liked to call a "jerk." I could tell that Liam wasn't the same Liam I had grown up with, but I wanted him to be, so I ignored all the red flags.

Papi's frown got frownier. "You shouldn't talk to him," he added sternly.

"But I have to talk to him, Papi," I replied, a bit startled "He used to be my best friend. I have to reconnect with him."

Grandpa laughed. Then he shrugged. I knew that was all the warning I was going to get.

Liam and I kept talking. He didn't seem like he was bad or annoying or rude. Or a jerk. It was like we were neighbors again, falling into comfortable and safe old patterns. Liam and I had agreed to see a movie a few days after our first Skype date, but the night before, I was sleeping at my grandparents' house and couldn't wait to see him, so I strapped my dog Jesse up to go for a walk, and together we trekked up the giant hill to go to Liam's house.

I got to the street and tried to pick out which exact house was his. I had to dig back into my memory bank and remember an old birthday of Liam's where his parents got a pet shop to bring over a bunch of reptiles (Liam loved snakes), and had all of us kids play with the reptiles in the front yard. I remembered that yard. Liam's house was the corner house. I knocked. He answered the door. Liam!

It was a warm evening and he offered to walk me back to my grandparents' house, and we caught up. I learned about his new friends and where they lived in the city. I learned about the girls I had gone to elementary school with and what they were up to. At the bottom of the giant hill, he kissed me. It was short and sweet, yet also a bit weird. Who even was this person anyway?

But I liked it. Or at least, I forced myself to like it. I forced myself to like him. I remember going to sleeping thinking, Hmm, this could be some Nicholas Sparks book kind of situation. This actually could be a thing between us. Long-lost besties fall into torrid romance! That would be SO CUTE.

So Liam and I started hanging out after that. But . . . the more time I spent with him, the more I realized it wasn't a Nicholas Sparks story at all. I actually didn't like him anymore—I just liked the idea of the magic of our childhood crush still being alive. I didn't know what to do. I started feeling guilty because my grandpa had warned me and I hadn't listened. Liam and I actually had literally nothing in common, and he started showing that he really was kind of rude. I still thought, though, that I had to keep this person in my life simply because I'd been so close to him before.

Liam started getting familiar with my new girlfriends from my new city, and after a few movie dates with the squad, I found out that Liam had gone on a movie date on his own time with one of my BEST FRIENDS.

That's when I decided maybe I didn't need to keep this person in my life, after all. Maybe he wasn't a good person. Maybe Papi was right. Maybe he was just a jerk.

So I faded away from Liam, and all my hopes of people staying the same for life were gone.

Well, as it turned out, Liam grew up to get a job working at a local weed dispensary in the same town we grew up in. I can't see how he has much of a future, so I guess some things work out for the best.

And the moral of the story is . . . sometimes it's a lot better to just have sweet and happy memories of your childhood crushes. Just because someone is adorable when they're six doesn't mean they'll stay adorable when they're sixteen!

When I was in high school, I was not a party person. I was never invited to parties, I never attended them, and I didn't even know they were even going on . . . until I met JC.

I'd always known about JC. In fact, years after I had officially met him in high school, my mom found a photo of me from the 2002 chess club, where I was smiling and holding my award for obviously beating everyone in chess . . . and JC was photobombing in the back left, and he was looking at me! BTW, yes. Yes, I was in chess club!

I got familiar with JC my junior year. He was tall—seven feet tall, to be exact, a senior boy, and the star of our school's basketball team. My school had a funny way of deciding if you were popular or not. Basically, anyone who was really different was actually really popular. If you had a mental disability, the popular kids would make you feel like the coolest kid in town. If you had no money to hang with the popular kids, but your personality was gold, guess what? You were in! This meant that if you were a seven-foot-tall white kid who was a whiz on the basketball courts, there was a highly excellent chance you would be popular.

Everyone loved JC. He was the MAN. I mean, you couldn't miss him around campus. The teachers loved him. The faculty loved him. The faculty's pets loved him. And when I started dating him, it meant that everyone loved me too.

Dating JC introduced me to a whole new world of experiences. Suddenly I went from quietly doing my own thing in the corner, being friendly to everyone but never being the center of attention,

to being the talk of the school. I was JC's GIRLFRIEND—me, a lowly junior girl! Teachers I didn't even ever have were suddenly interested in my life and yelling funny jokes at me through passing period like I had been born into their immediate family.

Suddenly I was going to basketball games, having friends when I got there (weird), and being invited to parties. Like, the raging kind. The "parents gone for the weekend" kind.

To be honest, these parties all sucked. I think I figured out junior year of high school that while I occasionally enjoy dressing up to look hot AF and slaying the crowd with my rare, glo'd-up existence, parties really don't mean that much to me. FOMO wasn't as important as sleep . . . beautiful precious sleeeeep.

I remember JC made me feel older. He had a car, and it was actually a nice car. It was one of those boxy ones that looked like an ice cube, and I know everyone hates those . . . but back in high school, when you were either driving a 1988 Honda Civic with a crack in the back window or not driving anything, the ice cube was pretty sweet.

I didn't have my license or even my permit, but when it was late at night sometimes JC would let me practice driving around my neighborhood. I never told my parents, but he was the first person who taught me how to drive!

JC and I would drive his ice cube to our old elementary schools and make out in his car. Note: If you ever want to hook up in a car—do it at elementary schools. But, like, don't tell anyone I told you that. However, even though we got frisky in his car, I never felt ready to have sex with him. He asked me a ton of ways and even tried to pressure me with some sassy comments, and eventually gave up on having full-on sex and started asking for compromises—you can use your creativity to think of what they may have been. I kept saying no, though, because for one thing, the chance of getting pregnant was just way too scary. And for another, I just didn't feel ready.

I tried my hardest to fit into JC's lifestyle. I watched hours of college basketball on his uncomfortable family-room couch while trying to talk sports with his die-hard dad, who clearly wanted JC to become an NBA star more than his son did. I did crafts with his mom and rode with her to some of his games. I pretended to care about JC's new see-through-plastic speaker system he installed in his bedroom and sat with him on his bed for a full twenty-two minutes while we listened to what was the worst Creed album of all time . . . and jammed to it wholeheartedly.

Things with JC started to fade quickly, after around two months. I knew something felt weird, especially the one time I was sitting on the same couch I watched college basketball with his dad on, and I started noticing JC texting his ex behind my back. When I saw a text from her saying, "I can't wait to see you," that's when I immediately knew what was going on.

Well, just as I suspected, JC ended up cheating on me. But the craziest thing was, I wasn't even mad! Of course I cried the second that we ended things. I even called him in public to try to stop it from ending and made an absolute fool of myself, crying hysterically on the phone in front of a twenty-four-hour fitness center and Jamba Juice store while my grandma waited in the car . . . but then a few hours later I realized how absolutely crazy I was for caring about him when our relationship only consisted of parties, me getting peer-pressured to drink and have sex, kissing in cars, and watching endless amounts of college basketball on that damn couch. Seriously??? I was going to spend my time crying over that?!

I knew I had to be quick about straightening out my feelings on the situation, since this relationship was such a public thing around the school. My status had been elevated to a weird position, and I knew that if I went back to school acting sad about this, I'd forevermore be the stupid junior girl who was cheated on by JC. I'd be the talk of the whole senior class.

So what did I do? I fixed myself up and returned to school confident as ever. I made sure to look HOT, and when people asked about me and JC, I straight-up told them that we broke up.

Heads up: When you go through a breakup, suddenly the other 90 percent of the population (that didn't even care about your existence pre-relationship) suddenly tries to act like your caring bestie to get all the tea from you when the relationship ends. There's going to be a lot of randoms who were never there for you to congratulate you on the start of your relationship, never there for you for the ups and downs in your relationship, but somehow want to be there for the fall of your relationship. For some reason, lots of people only care about negativity.

Guess what? You don't have to tell them anything. When my relationship with JC ended, I obviously stopped having my family drive me to his house and his games all the time, so naturally my parents kept asking, "Where is JC?" and, "What happened?!" I didn't even tell THEM anything until months later!

You don't owe anyone anything, and you especially don't owe people who were never even there for you anything. They only want the information so they can talk about it later with their friends.

Now, I knew back then that I didn't owe anyone anything—but I also knew that one thing is for sure: If you are going through something that another person is involved in, it's always better for you to speak your truth before you let them decide the course of the way the story will go. Let's say Sally saw a dress that was most definitely red, but sometimes Sally would go around telling people it was actually light pink and then now the dress was blue and you're actually crazy for thinking it was ever red. Got that? You can't have everyone on your side, because some people are stupid and will believe anything Sally tells them and there's nothing we can do about them, but for the people who actually can decide right from wrong, it's better to just tell the truth and stop at where you're comfortable.

So I told them. JC and I broke up. That was the "red" of the story, and the truth.

They all would act shocked and ask if I was okay.

I said, "Of course I'm okay! It's not that big of a deal!" and smiled and moved the conversation on. Well, a week later, JC was already back together with his ex from another school. That's when the second wave of snoopy kids came.

When people asked about it, clearly hinting that JC had cheated on me, since one week wasn't that long to rekindle a relationship all the way to "official," I gave them exactly what they were thinking I would never have the guts to say. I looked them straight in the eye and said, "JC cheated on me." Then I'd smile nonchalantly. "But that's okay! I'm not mad, because he's happy, and that's all that matters."

I controlled the reaction. All I did was stay calm—absolutely no drama!—and tell the truth. He did cheat, and I wasn't about to cover for him. No way! But the fact that I acted totally fine about things was what made people quickly move on from what could have been a major drama situation. I probably sounded crazy, because for someone who was cheated on, I really wasn't that fazed. But I think it was me finally realizing that crying over a relationship forever wastes so much time, and really, the time spent crying could be time spent realizing your worth. So I didn't once cry about it at school. I didn't say one bad word about JC and his ex-girlfriend-now-his-girlfriend-again, and that was the best thing I could have done, because you know what happened? People totally respected me for that!

As a result, his friends lit into him playfully and threw me a lot of respect, because I'd been so honest about what happened. A lot of them stayed friends with me, and since I was on the track team with lots of his friends, I eventually got to earn their friendship on my own.

JC went on to graduate, and I went on to remaining friends with all the senior friends he introduced me to. I went about the year still respected by them all!

If something like this happens to you, my advice is to fix the emotions you're going through when you're back at home. Cry it out in the privacy of your bedroom. Cry it out with your girlfriends who'll give you sympathy and support. Get out as much of the initial sad emotion as you can, but then dry your eyes. Put some ice cubes on them so you aren't puffy, and wash your face before bed. Apply a fab new shade of lipstick and wear something cute to school the next day. Make yourself feel amazing again.

Go to school with your head held high as if you don't have a care in the world. The best thing is that everyone will be expecting you to be a puddle on the floor, sobbing into an entire box of tissues at the back of the classroom, but you're not going to give them that. Don't give them the satisfaction of a drama. Stun them with how well you're handling yourself! It's a really powerful feeling to prove them all wrong, and you'll totally know you're doing it, because you'll see the shocked looks on their faces!

Here's another thing I learned after that breakup: It's kind of fun to reinvent yourself after a guy knocks you down. It's fun to show people how strong you are, and it's the best feeling showing up at school looking all hot and fantastic when everyone is expecting to see you looking like 2007 Britney Spears.

THREE WAYS TO ABSOLUTELY KILL YOUR FIRST DAY BACK FROM A BREAKUP

 Know what you're getting into and prepare your quick and witty comebacks.

There are going to be people trying to get any info they can on your breakup. Literally half the school turns into TMZ intern reporters. Be prepared for that! Don't let them see any tears behind your eyes when they ask, "What happened?" with fake concern dripping from their voices. Just say, "We broke up. That's what happened. I have to go now," and watch them trip on their words as you sashay away to the frozen-yogurt line. Byeee!

 **Wear something special.**

Going through the first day back from a breakup doesn't mean you have to go shopping the night before and find some magical red Dior gown and heels to wear to school. We're not going for new here, we're going for "WHAM-BAM." We're going for "Whoa,

I haven't seen Eva looking this good in a while." Were going for "Whoa, I didn't even notice her eyes were bright green until today!" Things like THAT. Have you ever gone to school one day and realized the girl who's worn glasses and a hat since she popped out of the womb has suddenly decided to switch things up for the day and DAMN WTF SHE IS HOT?! That's what we're going for!

So what is something you rarely wear? What about that black leather jacket you forgot about that sits in the back of your closet? What about those wedge heels you wore to a banquet a few months ago? What about your mom's nude lipstick you think could look good on you if you tried it out? Find something you own that you can reinvent into a symbol of a new you, model it in front of your mirror, and if it makes you feel fancy, that's what you're going to rock the next day!

 Remember that this is only one of the many relationships you will have.

I know sometimes we all like to wallow in our loneliness and potato-ness for fun. That sounds really sad, but trust me, we all do it. Of course, I do it too.

If you find yourself in this place, there is one thing you must not do: Go on Twitter.

These are some of the sad tweets I've

definitely thought about sending before and am so glad I didn't:

- 👁 *I have about ten open Safari pages for the search "munchkin cat" on Craigslist OC. Trying to find my cat a couple of friends . . . I will die alone.*

- 👁 *It's a Friday night and I didn't even realize it was the weekend until I checked Facebook and saw all my friends having fun without me.*

- 👁 *I love having a small amount of friends because it means less people I have to stealthily hide my good snacks from when we're all together.*

It's easy to poke fun at how we all feel a little lonely and friendless sometimes, but the thing to remember is that even though you may be single now or for a few months or a few years, there will be many people passing in and out your life, and your ex is just one of them. Moving on doesn't have to happen instantly for some people, but it's definitely important to realize there's a time for moving on and it **will** come. So for now, just smile for the good memories you had while with that person, and look forward to forming new memories with new people!

GIRL TALK

When I was in high school, not a single person came out. Everybody knew who was gay, but no one talked about it. It's not like coming out would mean they would get bullied. My school was actually really accepting! It was more just that nobody felt the need to really "come out" like they do more today. People came out when they were ready, and their way of coming out was just them publicly dating someone of the same sex. Nowadays, coming out to more than just your family means a lot more. With all the coming-out videos on YouTube, telling people you're gay sometimes seems like more of an announcement than just a feeling.

I always knew I liked girls. I always was attracted to them and was very open about it. If I saw a girl I liked, I would walk right up to her and tell her, "I think you're hot. Let's hook up . . . but really . . . like . . . I'm down," which is funny, because my approach with girls was actually ten times more confident than my approach with guys.

The reason I was so direct with girls was because with guys, it's almost expected that every girl is meant to be "straight." If a guy sees a girl and likes her, he'll almost always try to flirt with her. But with girls, you never know who feels what, and at the time, nearly every girl in my life would have called herself straight.

The thing was, my high school life was filled with a lot of really great girls. I had this amazing friend Michelle, and we were in yearbook together. She was part of my friend group and I always thought she was gorgeous. We would always have little moments together where I thought she might be into me, but nothing big ever happened. When you're seventeen years old in 2011, making moves on people of the same sex as you would have been too bold for most people.

One night we were all at Taco Bell playing truth or dare, and my guy friend Tyler asked Michelle if she would ever hook up with a girl. The whole table laughed, as if hooking up with a girl would be some funny joke. She looked at him and said, "Of course I would!" The whole table erupted into a big "OOOOOOHHHHHHH" and someone's Baja Blast Freeze got knocked over on the table. Tyler then asked, "Would you ever hook up with Eva?" Michelle goes, "Duh. I think Eva is so hot." My heart stopped. We both looked at each other and smiled. Michelle was down. *Yes.*

I spent the next three years trying to see where things might go with Michelle, but soon she got a boyfriend and faded away from my life.

Anyway, in my high school, people who were gay were loved because of how honest they were with themselves—but girls who were bisexual were looked at as "sluts" who were just "confused."

A number of the girls who were out as "bisexuals" turned the label into a bad thing. They did drugs and hooked up with dirty boys from other neighboring schools and wore trashy clothes. Even though I knew how I felt, I never wanted to say the word *bisexual*—not because I was scared of being labeled weird for it, but because other people had pre-conceived notions about what the term meant to them.

I have spent all of my life being totally open about how I felt. If anyone ever asked, I never lied to them. Especially girls. I wanted every girl to know I was bi, just in case they secretly were too. Options of girls who liked girls were slim at my school, so I had to be honest if I was ever going to find a girl for me!

What I realized was that for girls at my high school, everyone thought that if you'd say, "OMG I love you. You're so amazing. Let's hang out," it was just girl talk. That's what straight girl best friends say to each other, after all. I would have to be more blatantly obvious with girls than guys, because so many people just assumed I was kidding, especially because I was only dating boys. But the only reason I was dating just boys was because nobody ever believed me that I liked girls!

I didn't know how to make it clear that sometimes it **wasn't** just girl talk.

At the time I was in school, nobody took people who were bi seriously. They would tell me, "You can't just go around saying you're a bisexual because you would kiss a girl." They would almost try to convince me that I was wrong about myself. But they were just looking for a reason to start an argument. I always knew what being bi meant, but never knew what bi really *felt* like. All I knew was that I knew what I wanted.

So many moments happened growing up that I still to this day don't understand. I had a best friend that led me through the most confusing moments. Like getting naked in expensive lingerie shops and helping each other zip into half-cup lace bras. Judging open-crotch thongs in the mirror with her. Cuddling in bed with the lights off in lingerie and taking sexy photos of each other. Making out at every party we ended up at.

We were so gay for each other for literal years that even both my ex-boyfriends at the time would joke around and say, "I think I'm dating a lesbian." One even seriously sat me down and was like, "Um, Eva . . . are you gay?" I was like, yes. Duh.

I was never scared to come out. I didn't think it was a big deal or a shock, and if it was a big deal to anyone, then I didn't want them in my life anyway. Being bi was just me, and it felt normal.

So while all my friends knew this and

basically shrugged about it, because to me it was no big deal, I think my sharing it on social media was a bit of a shock to many of my viewers! I never "came out" online, because I just didn't know how to do it. I knew that my story would help people, but, like a lot of things in my life, I wanted it to be perfect. When I care about things, I take way way *way* too long to say them, because I want them to be perfect! Well, if I kept on the path of being scared to come out because it wouldn't be a perfect coming-out announcement video, I would have never come out.

But here's what happened: I was in Australia one night with my also-bisexual girlfriend, and she got me really drunk on a bottle of champagne. We were discussing how dumb it was that being bi is considered a joke to people, and I took out my phone and started drunk-tweeting my feelings. I was JUST trying to say my feelings and that's it! I went to bed and the next morning this was all over Twitter.

> **Lifestyle Vlogger @LifeAsEva Reveals She's Bisexual**

I was getting comments like "OMG you're so brave" and "You've inspired me to come out too." I started a movement in my sleep! I didn't even think I was coming out when I tweeted! I realized I had made a drunk "mistake," but actually it wasn't a mistake. In fact, I'm glad it happened, because if I hadn't have gotten drunk with my bi girlfriend, I would have never have had the courage to say what I did in the most eloquent, easy way possible.

Coming out for me wasn't a monumental moment. I could just as easily have done it when sitting in the bathroom pooping! I know I would have said the exact same thing eventually. I just wanted to tell people, and I realized in retrospect that Twitter was the best place to do it, as it was kind of perfect the way that conversation spontaneously happened. Not being totally open just made it a bigger deal than it actually is. If I hadn't stated that I was truly bisexual, people would still think I was joking if I mentioned how hot a girl was!

The reason I've been so open about things growing up is that it's better to be out and owning it than to be too scared to be who you are. I took ownership of my feelings and my deeds. I always made jokes—for me, making fun of myself and not hiding it was the way to go. If I got a bad haircut, I owned it. If I broke up with someone, I said why. If I failed, I accepted it.

So you might think that being honest about tough topics is scary, but it actually isn't. It's empowering. And it's never as scary as what people are saying behind your back if you aren't honest. I mean, everyone will talk about you, no matter what. And I knew that if people were talking about me, it didn't matter. I liked who I was. I liked liking boys and girls. I never thought I was weird or different for liking girls, and I knew that if anyone ever came to me trying to convince me I was wrong, I'd just brush them aside.

Still, I'm openly bi but still lost. I have so many questions. When will girls start hitting on me? Do I just not look approachable to girls? Do people still not believe me? Do I even know how to flirt with a girl? If I do get a girl, will I be like a reborn-again virgin who doesn't know anything???

Who knows what will happen? I'm still waiting for a girl to even look at me. Regardless, whatever's out there, I'm ready for it!

EVEN THOUGH I was depressed and in hoodies a lot of sophomore year, I still wanted to create a look that you can wear when you want to be in comfy, simple clothes, but still cute! A plain over-size tee with boyfriend jeans can be glammed up with just running shoes and an over-sized coat! Yet you're still super warm and cozy.

SOPHOMORE YEAR

CHAPTER 4

Glo—Up Level, SOPHOMORE STYLE

kay, so we all know by now that freshman year was the year of the scene-kid style. Well, sophomore year, my style dramatically changed. Seriously. I went from death metal and electronic punk "pig squealing" to "Hi, my name is Hannah and I work at the local Hollister store!"

Sophomore year was when I started really paying attention to all the people around me at school, looking at how they dressed, and I figured out that the cool kids wore a certain style that was just plain enough to be plain, but cool enough to be cool. It was like this beachy California-girl style that I once attempted back in junior high but failed at. I thought it was more fitting for me to give it a go, since being a scene kid was kind of over for me.

Unfortunately, achieving this rich-kid Orange County look was actually really freaking hard. For some reason, even though the clothes that many of my classmates were wearing seemed pretty easy to copy (basic fitted tees and whitewash flare jeans), I couldn't seem to look anywhere as hot and "all-American" as they did. Maybe it was because I didn't have boobs. Or nice skin . . . or nice hair. Or maybe I just wasn't wearing the look right?

Anyhoo, I ended up failing and falling somewhere in between Old Navy model and hand-me-down queen. I couldn't afford to go shopping at the stores my class-mates were shopping at, so I had to work a little harder to find things at the thrift store and on clearance racks that could pass as similar. Sometimes it worked, and sometimes it didn't. Unfortunately, I think it failed more than succeeded, because I can only find photos of me from sopho-more year looking absolutely busted.

Most of sophomore year, I practically lived in dance shorts, and I ended up collecting so many hoodies that I needed two whole drawers and fifteen hangers to hang them all up!

I also had these snazzy butterfly ear-rings that, apparently, I wore everywhere. Probably because I figured out that my hair was way too crazy to straighten every day and make look good, so instead, why shouldn't I just straighten the front bang part and pin the rest up inside a hat? So I did that look, and the hair in the hat went unwashed for days and the hair left out was damaged to shreds.

I think overall, I just really wanted to fit in like the other kids in my school. It wasn't because I was insecure with how I looked, or that I wanted to look like the kids in school to make them like me, but more because keeping up with the scene style was hard work, and I needed to find a look that seemed effortless and easy. I wanted to blend in, because style takes time, and honestly, with the depression I was going

through, fashion was the last thing I was thinking about. A lot of the time during this year in school, I looked kind of sad. I looked tired and lost. Stress definitely got to me, and I didn't know how to take care of my-self when it happened!

MY BEST TIPS FOR HOW TO TAKE CARE OF YOURSELF WHEN YOU'RE STRESSED—SO YOU DON'T END UP LOOKING LIKE ME SOPHOMORE YEAR (HA-HA-HA)

Take Care of Your Body

One thing I wish I did better sophomore year was take care of my body!

I grew up in a house where everyone in the family would share ONE tiny bathroom that was always messy and barely had any space to breathe. Because of that, I always wanted to just get in and out and never wanted to pamper myself. Now, I'm NOT the type of girl to exfoliate my entire body three times a week, bathe myself in flower petals, and deep-condition my hair as much as the bottle tells me I should, but I now know the importance of UPKEEP.

Here's what I'm saying: I can get by a

solid two weeks without shaving my legs and a good three days without putting deodorant on before I start smelling like a dead seal and looking like a woolly mammoth. Everyone has their own expiration date on different parts of their beauty regimen. You might know that you wouldn't even last for two hours without applying deodorant (honestly, that's me on a lot of hot days). Only you know your body, and no one person can give you a routine on how to take care of it. Hair gets oily at different paces for different people, and toenail polish chips at your own rate (for me, it's usually the day after a pedicure!).

Do I recommend that strategy? No, I do not!

Give your body some ME time in the shower or bathtub.

When you know it's time to take care of yourself, don't start letting that ever-so-important timer go on sleep mode. I do it sometimes when I get too stressed out with more important things. I work and I work and I forget "Hey, wait a second, I haven't showered in four days!" Seriously . . . it happens. (I'm going on day two here while writing this!)

Those little slipups MESS with your body. They wear you down physically and psychologically. Get yourself clean. It's important to wash your face before bed and make sure no dirt is collecting be-

hind your ears for six weeks. Just like your parents may tidy up the house every day, and then every once in a while bust out the bleach and the bottles of multicolored cleansers and scrub the tub and the windowsills and then broom out all the dust bunnies lurking under the beds, you need to look at your body the same way. If you just "tidy up" your body for your entire life, think about how much dirt and who knows what is building up in places you don't want to think about!

So no matter what kind of state of mind you're in, shower, scrub yourself as much as you can, and please take a Q-tip and clean out those weird crevices of your belly button and ears. Trust me, you're gonna find some stuff in places you definitely thought were clean.

Put ice cubes on your eyes so you don't have bags underneath them.

One thing that I read in a magazine back when I was in high school was that you could take an ice cube and put it under your eyes, and it will reduce your dark circles and make you look more awake. So, every morning that I could, I would go into my freezer before school, get an ice cube, and hold it to under my eyes for thirty seconds. It made me feel SO alive, awake, and refreshed, and it really did make my eyes look better in the morning!

If you feel like cuddling up in a sweater, here are some other, more stylish options!

I had an extensive collection of hoodies my sophomore year, which I think is SO funny looking back on! They were all I really wore—I had SO MANY. When you're stressed out, it's easy to go to an easy outfit to throw on, because you don't have to think about it and you know it's going to work. I'm all about my sweaters and leggings, but I wish I knew back then that there were ways to achieve that comfy, effortless style without looking plain. Here's an outfit I wish I knew would look just as cute and cost just as much back in sophomore year.

 Get enough sleep.

I hear this ALL the time, and don't listen to it as often as I should. Sleep is important and it's so, so valuable. I know sometimes we want to do everything and, with me, that feeling definitely gets more intense at night. But the thing that makes me stop whatever I'm doing and go to sleep is knowing that anything that can be done in the middle of the night can also be done in the early morning—and that resting and waking up early feels so good when you know you have a full day ahead of you and you've already started your day while the rest of the world is sleeping.

CHAPTER 5

FRIENDS

GIRL SQUADS

've always been the type of person to treat everyone equally right off the bat. I've never been one of those girls who just looks at someone and decides, "I'm going to be standoffish to them." It makes NO sense to me, and even to this day, I still come across girls who immediately decide that they're going to be mean to someone new.

It sucked, because if I ever did find myself in a squad of girls, the girls would all start being really influenced by the leader of the group, who was usually mean, and I just didn't want to be a part of that so I never really fit in.

I remember being in my first real "girl squad" in elementary school, and watching the main leader of the group force this sad, nerdy kid to run into the girls' bathroom and get her toilet paper, and he did it over and over again because he liked her so much. On our last day of elementary school, she got our squad to hide in the second-grade bathroom to scare little kids into thinking there was a ghost in the stall. That was when I realized maybe this squad wasn't for me.

I had grown up, just barely getting by, by tagging along with the neighborhood kids and riding my bike behind them close enough to look included but just far enough to look normal. The problem for me was that I would make friends with everyone by being nice, but never had a best friend to call my own.

I never really truly found **my** squad. I

bounced from best friend to best friend, but most of my best friends belonged to bigger squads with other girlfriends in them that I never got the chance to be friends with, so I never really got invited to true squad things.

I don't know why my life was always like that. It was always like I was someone's second-best friend, but never anyone's first choice. And when I did manage to score a best friend, they'd usually turn out crazy. Let me TELL you, moms actually do know best when they get bad vibes from people, even young children, because every time I'd befriend someone a little crazy, my mom would tell me instantly how she felt about them. Of course I'd be like, "OK MOM YOU'RE CRAZY! THEY'RE THE BEST!" but then a year later I'd be like, "Oh . . . yeah, you were right." Oops.

I learned that when you're young you can get away with not having a best friend. You can get away with not having a squad to hang with at night, and you never have to worry about who you can go to see a movie with, or who to go to dances with. Those aren't even questions we had to worry about as kids!

(Ah, the good old days, when the worst problem was the crimson crayon gone missing!)

Even as I got older, I was always the random one in the prom group that wiggled her way onto the party bus. I had a birthday in the middle of summer, so I never had friends around to celebrate my birthday with.

I felt like I'd always been a fish floating around in the ocean whose rest of her fish family took one wrong turn in a current and got themselves extinct, and now I was just swimming around helplessly, looking for another fish that related to me in any sort of way.

My girl squad from elementary school, the same one that tormented both second graders and crazy-in-love little boys in bathroom stalls, all went their separate ways in high school. Some became cheerleaders, some joined choir, some moved out of the area . . . but most of them became hot and popular. Not me. I, for some reason, didn't get whatever genes they were passing around. It took me a few more years before I figured out how to even get somewhere as cool as they all were right after entering high school.

When high school started, I had no squad. No group to call mine. No friend to run to when the lunch bell rang. I had to think fast, so I found myself falling into the quickest and coolest friend group that would take me in: the scene kids.

Over that first year of school, I saw how the scene kids were cool . . . almost in their own little bubble. It was like a whole other culture with them. In lots of high schools, different groups are competing to be the coolest in school, but not the scene kids. The scene kids were too busy trying to keep up with the whole WORLD to be the coolest in school.

Being friends with the scene kids was the first time I really got a taste of the "online world," the world outside of just my hometown friends' accounts. A big part of being a cool scene kid was that you'd have tons of online friends who you'd never met before—which at first made no sense to me, because why would you want to be friends with a ton of strangers you'll never meet—but I quickly found out that in the scene world, more friends meant more people liked you. It showed status. The more friends you had added, the cooler you were.

I noticed that all the scene girls had a super unique look to them. Their hair was cool. Cooler than anything my mom would ever let me do. Some girls had blue hair, some had fluffy green hair with rattails and dyed patterns in it. Their eyeliner was thick and made their eyes look ginormous. Their clothes were tiny and colorful and made them look like dolls.

No group is complete without a leader, and the leader of the scene kids at my school was Janet, a hot, cool Asian girl who seemed like she had it all

figured out. She had one of those totally amazing, laid-back moms that for sure smoked weed, and so Janet got to dye her hair any color she wanted. I was super jealous. My mom wouldn't let me dye my hair until I turned eighteen. Janet gave me all the style inspiration I could ask for. She always ripped her clothes in the most perfect way, and picked the best suspenders, clip-in extensions, and hair bows to complement them.

I tried my best to do the look. I tried to layer my hair in the bathroom. I didn't have eyeliner, so I couldn't ever try out that look, but I did the best I could by buying ALL of my clothes at Hot Topic. All I wanted were  band tees, but band tees were for some reason really freaking expensive, so I really only ended up collecting around two or three. I still remember my DEVIL WEARS PRADA shirt with an evil gingerbread man on it, which I bought about three sizes too small and wore everywhere until it faded, then continued to wear it. And when Hot Topic was too expensive for my budget, I found a couple of band tees at the Goodwill thrift store and started to wear those, never even knowing that in the scene world, LITERALLY nobody liked the bands whose merch I was wearing, even though I thought I'd definitely fit in with these new shirts.

Once I had my scene look as down as I could nail it, I started doing scene kid things, like adding a bunch of randoms on MySpace and even taking pictures of "signs" (this was a weird trend where you'd write a name on paper and hold it up for a picture) for random girls I didn't know who were probably twenty-five years older than me.

Back then, I was super into the scene culture—but not just the online part of it. I loved the music. I don't know if I really did enjoy it or if I taught myself to love it so I could fit in, but looking back, I still remember the lyrics to more than half of the screamo music I listened to. I can even still belt it out, although every single person I've proudly done it in front of has looked at me like I was on drugs.

It was certainly an interesting group, but I loved my friends. I finally had a squad and we were happy. They all showed me new music, and took me to places I'd never been before, like concerts.

And like the Tunnels underneath the city.

THE TUNNELS

Here's a story my parents probably don't know . . .

Ever do something and then look back and laugh, thinking, Wow, why did I do *that*? It's not like you regret it, exactly, but you just can't help but think to yourself, Why . . . just *why*. For me, that's the Tunnels.

I got introduced to the Tunnels by my new, cool, scene-kid squad. We were hanging out at the local movie theater (the hot spot for high school kids), when I suddenly heard a kid yell out, "Hey, let's go to the Tunnels!" Now, as you've come to realize, I'm not the kid in the squad that's really there for much. I was kind of the side piece just following along in the back that nobody seemed to mind. I brought some good jokes to the group, but I missed out on like 90 percent of my squad's activities, since most of them lived in the same neighborhood and I lived far away from them. And there were always new kids coming in and out of the squad that everyone seemed to know but me, even though these new kids would be from a school seven miles away. So when this kid (who I'd never seen before) yelled out, "Hey, let's go to the Tunnels!" and everyone got excited and started getting up saying, "Yeah!" and, "Oh my God, yes, let's go!" I just went with the flow. Yeah! The Tunnels? What's that again?

A few dirt trails and a sketchy gate hop into an empty reservoir later, we found ourselves in front of a massive hole. A hole big enough to drive a car through. The hole was dark and scary, and I'd never seen anything like it before in my life. This must have been the Tunnels.

It was basically just a giant sewer hole. My friends explained to me that if you went into the hole—or the Tunnels— it would lead into a two-mile-long passageway that spanned underneath the city. It started where we were standing, by the movie theater, and ended up in a nearby suburban town's dried-up lake.

I looked at Janet. Were we seriously going to do this? She smiled deviously and started explaining what the Tunnels were all about to me, as if we were at the beginning of some *Mission: Impossible* movie and she was giving me my assignment.

"The Tunnels have no light and it's pitch-black the whole way through," Janet told me, "and there's always a bit of sewer water at the bottom. When it rains, the water gets deeper and it's super fun. The walls are lined with graffiti and the only way to see anything is to use a flashlight! Oh, and some say it's haunted . . . by the shadow people."

WHO WOULD DO THIS?

Me.

Well, my new squad introduced me to the Tunnels, and together nearly every weekend we'd go through them for fun. We'd use flashlights to maneuver our way through the sewage and laugh through all the smells. We'd meet some interesting people along the way to the other end of the Tunnels, but fortunately everyone was always really nice and young like us. To be honest, it was a pretty weird thing to do, looking back, but it was also something really, really fun.

I never did see the shadow people, though.

Despite all the extremely weird things we got ourselves into, the coolest thing about my new squad was that they didn't drink or do drugs. I really loved that about them, because I really didn't feel a need to do any of that stuff, and they kept me on the right path. We all looked out for each other. We had so much fun making all these insane memories, living life like crazy kids, and we did it all sober. I was really proud of that. I knew from the beginning that drugs were SO not my thing, and to find a group of people that also didn't care to try them out was extremely special to me.

WHEN GROUP DYNAMICS OF THE GIRL SQUADS GO BAD . . .

or, Jenny and the Dance Team

Dance has been a part of my life since I was three. I grew up on a ton of performing teams and was always traveling around California, dancing, singing, and performing for crowds. I was like a street monkey, only with . . . no, I was pretty much a street monkey.

I was in absolute love with dance, but being Eva, I was also in love with 39,432,443 other things just as much. I was just trying to figure out where I belonged! Soccer had shared the same time of my life as dance, and it was way cheaper, so I started playing soccer instead of dancing.

I got really into soccer for nearly eleven years of my life, and when high school approached, I realized that I wanted to get back into dancing. But because I'd stopped dancing for a solid few years, I had unwittingly lost a lot of my flexibility . . . and the ability to do anything cool. I quickly found out that I legit sucked. It was the summer before freshman year, and tryouts for the dance team were going on. I was cut so fast, I didn't even know what was coming to me. It was a slap in the face. I had a long way to go before I was at the level I thought I already was on.

When freshman year started, and I was getting familiar with my class schedule, this is what I had to deal with every day:

Eva's Class Schedule

1ST PERIOD:	Dance 1
2ND PERIOD:	US History
3RD PERIOD:	Drama
4TH PERIOD:	Honors English
5TH PERIOD:	Algebra 1
6TH PERIOD:	Earth Science

I was also getting familiar with Jenny. Because I sucked at dance now, I had to endure a full year of being in what we called Dance 1 at my school. It was essentially a basic-level P.E. class that anyone could take to get out of running miles and enduring two weeks' worth of swim class. It was considered a joke class by most kids, and so people just took it to get an easy A and mess around with their friends. I, however, was in Dance 1 because I simply loved to dance, but in a sea of people who just didn't give a crap, I felt like a total outcast. There I was, trying so hard to get better, and yet I ended up feeling like an idiot when everyone else was laughing the class off.

Within the first couple days of Dance 1, I noticed Jenny. I mean, how could you miss her? She was poised. She came to dance class with her long brown hair in a high ponytail, and always had on her nude dance shoes that you could clearly tell had been through a lot of years of heavy weathering.

Jenny was clearly a dancer as well, but she was a hundred times better than me. She could do flawless turns and leg extensions I only dared to attempt in the comfort of my own bathroom. She danced for a studio (*ooh, a studio!*), and always had the trendiest collection of black dance clothes. Meanwhile, I was rocking my sister's old choir performance pants and my snazzy collection of free oversize band T-shirts that I'd collected over the past fourteen years of my life.

Plus, I was still a really goofy dancer and had a long way to go before I found my rhythm again, so I typically liked to hide in the back. But Jenny was always in the front. She took every challenge with ease and killed it. She inspired me to be like that too.

Jenny was also in my earth science class, and I instantly liked her, because I could tell she was a lot like me. Kind of lost on the friend situation, a little goofy, and she even wore high socks too with her regular outfits! SEE, MOM, I'm NOT crazy for wearing my purple soccer socks to school! It's going to be a thing. *Duh*.

After a couple days in the hell that was Dance 1, Jenny's talent was recog-nized, and she was moved up to Dance 3, which was the highest dance class you could get to before you made it onto the dance team. The dance team! Basically, it was my life goal to some day make it there. Getting on the dance team was basically the number one ticket to social elite club.

What I liked about Jenny was that even though she was such a great dancer, she was also a really sweet girl. Most girls at my school got cocky when they were better at things than others, but not Jenny. She helped me get better at dance, and danced with me when no one else would . . . which sounds cheesy but was actually literal!

Anyway, I've always wanted that fairy-tale-friend story where my mom and another mom magically had a baby in the same delivery room and became best friends and I went on to growing up alongside my since-diapers BFF. She was there for me, always. She would be my maid of honor at my wedding, giving me a crooked grin and a thumbs-up when I said my vows. Unfortunately, that never happened.

I had a lot of making up to do for all those many years of my life that I didn't grow up with a diaper bestie. Okay, so I didn't have a diaper bestie, but I did have the next best thing: a real best friend through thick and thin. Jenny.

Jenny became the first longtime, best girl, best friend I'd ever had. I told her everything, like about my intense crush on Ben, and even my depression I was going through at home (that I talk about on page 161). What especially made me feel better was that I knew Jenny had gone and was going through stuff as well, and that I wasn't alone with how I was feeling. We never had to share details; we just knew that we were both helping each other in some unspoken way.

Jenny and I filmed dumb lip-synching videos together in her bedroom. We had sleepovers. We even bought chalk and drew on the sidewalk during our summer break. We made our own fun!

Finding a friend like Jenny—someone who wasn't focused on being popular and moving up in the social world—was so great, because we could just focus on being teens, and not on getting caught up in all the popularity drama that other people were going through at the time.

Jenny and I had survived a lot together. Between me falling in love with, getting dumped by, and getting my emotions twisted around by Ben; failing classes and crying about them; getting bullied by mean girls on the cheer squad; and her crazy outrageous boyfriend fights, I thought Jenny and I could survive anything, until suddenly, it seemed like we couldn't.

Dance Team Drama

If you've ever been on a team, you know how hard it is to have a ton of people together in a group. Some people like each other. Some people don't. Some people take sides. Some feel caught in the middle between two sides who each are right and wrong at the same time. Some people start out with small egos and then get big egos and then morph into someone who is really out of control and upsetting the group.

When this happens, friendships can be severely tested.

So let me tell you what happened when—yay, me!—I made the dance team my senior year.

Finally! I was where I'd wanted to be after FOUR FREAKING years of rejection. I'm talking bloody feet, sprained ankles, and even quitting other things I was passionate about just to make this damn team. Years and years of having my mom drive me up the hill to the school, just to walk into the dance room and check "the list" only to realize yep, once again, I hadn't made it.

But finally, it was senior year. I checked the list and I HAD made it.

I was so happy! Plus, I was finally on the team alongside my best friend, Jenny!

A solid month went by on the dance team where everything seemed to be

A-OK, until all hell broke loose. See, the two dance captains, Raquel and Emma, were actually, to put it generously, high-key "personalities." The more popular one, Raquel, was always getting involved in the biggest dramas in the school.

The other one, Emma, who was less popular, was a taker, and I mean that literally. She took things, and even "borrowed" my history textbook and never gave it back, so I had to pay $80 to replace it. She even took articles of clothing that she knew didn't belong to her, like jackets on the floor. She had money. She didn't need that stuff. She just wanted to take it!

And of course, both of them were mortal enemies since KINDERGARTEN, ever since Raquel had had a party with the other girls from the studio and hadn't invited Emma. Seriously. This was the root of all the evil I'm about to tell you about.

I'm talking some CHILDISH (and potentially dangerous) stuff. Like them literally DROPPING each other off tables during partner work.

The dance team I'd wanted to be on more than anything in the whole world was led by two complete divas. What a letdown!

Then the fighting got so bad the team sort of got divided into two cliques. It was such a big mess, where one side would be pretty much all the popular girls on the dance team, led by Raquel, and the other would be the losers of the dance team, led by Emma. Don't ask why a squad with only twenty-one girls on it had to have winners and losers, but that's the kind of ridiculous drama that was going on!

Most of us didn't know what to do at first. Then these divas demanded that we pick a side. I was like, this is so dumb to even think about picking sides for some long-standing silly fight that I knew nothing about and didn't want to know anything about. To this day, the dance teacher said she respects me so much because I flat-out refused to pick sides. Because even in high school she knew I wasn't going to be a complete idiot!

Well, the fighting got even worse, so much so that one of the boys' coaches had to step in and tell us how stupid we were acting. Things finally came to a head when Raquel choreographed a dance behind our teacher's back, and it was way too sexually suggestive. Our teacher got in trouble too because she had seen the dance during rehearsals and should have stopped it, but she didn't. Some parents saw the dance during one of the basketball games and complained. Raquel got demoted from being one of the captains, and all of us got a bunch of privileges taken away. We were told that we were banned from performing at any of the basketball games for the rest of the year. When the season had just started.

The entire team got punished because of one diva's need for attention, and we were all devastated. Especially me, because a lot of the girls had been on the dance team for years, but there I was, finally on the team for my first and only year, and Raquel had taken away everything I'd worked for. And for what?

Raquel never apologized for the drama; she just looked pissed off when the coach gave us the bad news. That made the team even more polarized. Raquel's side felt like they had to stick with her because she was so popular, even though she'd let them down. There was this super weird air of saltiness floating through the divided team. Everyone was on edge. Finally, even Raquel got fed up and left the team.

That was Emma's chance to take over. Things got a little bit better, but her having such sticky fingers didn't exactly make her a leader we respected. In fact, she was just as bad as Raquel, but in different ways.

And what was far more devastating to me than not being allowed to perform at basketball games was when Emma took something a lot more important to me than a few books and a

couple of lipsticks. She took Jenny, my BFF.

Picking sides on the captain drama was kind of important if you wanted to be on the dance team. You see, the team got to dance in a number of full dances with the entire team in them. But when you were a captain, you got to choreograph small-group numbers, which were usually the more fun and more admired dances with cooler costumes. Basically, the more of the small group numbers you were in, the better. Well, when both the captains hated each other, they never chose each other to dance in their small groups. Girls that wanted to be in Raquel's small groups started kissing up to Raquel and legit bullying/ignoring/making fun of the girls that sided with Emma, and vice versa.

I didn't want to choose a side. I mean, on one side, I had a group of popular mean girls that were cliquey AF and weren't even nice to me BEFORE all this drama, and on the other side, I had Emma, the girl who took my best friend and took my things! If I picked Emma, the girls that already were mean to me on Raquel's side would only get meaner. So I didn't pick any side. Instead, I was caught in the middle.

But Jenny did pick a side. She picked Emma. Jenny was a pretty good dancer, and I'm pretty sure her mom told her to befriend Emma so that she could get good parts in dances, but I wasn't even that great of a dancer, so picking Emma to get good solo parts would have been pointless. Jenny wanted Emma for the benefits, but I just didn't care to be a part of the crazy drama that was going on. It would have been a grave mistake for me to have chosen either side—but I still didn't want to lose Jenny, so I kept trying to be amicable. During stretches before class, I'd sit next to Jenny . . . but then Jenny would move next to Emma, and I would move too, like a stupid little duckling chasing its mom until it finally fell into a gutter. It was this weird kind of triangle. I would be there for Jenny, and Jenny would be there for Emma, and the other girls siding with Raquel would think I was allying myself with Emma, when I was just spending more time with her because she was spending more time with Jenny!

I finally decided that none of this was worth it. This drama was childish and I realized that I definitely DID NOT have to pick a side! I So I gave up on trying to latch onto Jenny. I never talked to her about what she did, because I understood pretty clearly. I started walking around the school without her and Emma, and went my own way—the alone way.

There sure were a lot of lessons learned from this episode in my life— lessons I'm glad I learned in retrospect, but that were really tough to live through at the time:

 If two people have things they need to sort out, LET THEM HANDLE IT!

So many times one of the friends will try to drag anyone into it that they can, because they think having more people on their "side" makes them "win." In turn, it just creates a bigger mess. If it isn't your business, the best thing you can do is offer them one piece of advice: Get over it, make up, and move on.

 Sometimes your friends suprise you—and not in a good way.

I never thought Jenny would do that to me, but she did. She ended up liking Emma more than she liked me, for reasons that probably weren't the most well-thought-out, but that wasn't my fault and I couldn't live my life beating myself up over it.

 Be respectful of your team.

Don't be selfish! When you're on a team, your actions don't only reflect on you, but the whole group. Just like partying until 3 a.m. affects your entire team's performance the next day, starting drama you have no intentions of solving with another teammate is super disrespectful to everyone else that worked so hard to be involved with your team.

Overall, just be a good person. Don't start drama. If you see drama, try and help make peace! Don't allow yourself to be a follower. Be a leader and start your own team—aka #teamnoside or #teamgetoverit or #teamtherearemore importantissuesintheworld.

WHAT HAPPENS WHEN YOUR BESTIE ISN'T ANYMORE

It's really, really painful when someone can be a great friend for years, and then *wham*, your confidence is betrayed.

What happened on the dance team was only part of what went down with Jenny and me. Let me explain about Jenny's crazy outrageous boyfriend fights.

Around sophomore year of high school, Jenny started dating this boy who seemed really sweet. At first, I was all for their relationship. They spent almost every waking hour together, and they seemed attached at the hip. But by senior year, their relationship started getting weird. They would fight so much. I could see on Jenny's face there was a lot that she wasn't telling me anymore. They would fight so badly to the point

that even one day they fought on the very public steps to the cafeteria in front of everyone, and she even slapped him! Jenny stopped telling me things that she needed to let out. At the same time that she started fighting so badly with her boyfriend, she started hanging around this girl on the dance team that was co-captain, and a much better dancer than I was.

Cue the drama!

I didn't know exactly what was going on. All I knew was that I was most definitely being replaced, and every single day at school I was fading more and more into an unwanted, uncared-for third wheel. Like I wasn't even a third wheel. I was the spare tire kept underneath a mat in the trunk that will most likely never be used and that most car owners don't even know they have.

After four years of an incredible friendship with no drama ever, I just wasn't needed anymore.

My heart was hurting, but instead of fighting with Jenny, I figured I'd just let her have her new best friend. At least I was savvy enough (and hurt enough) to know that getting into it with her wasn't worth it. Jenny had made her decision. I wasn't even sure that she knew exactly what she had done to me. After all, I still had my friend Maddie from drama class and yearbook, and I'd been meaning to spend some more time with her, after all. So I stopped eating lunch with Jenny and Emma and started joining in on lunch with Maddie and the squad.

Senior year ended and I graduated. Jenny and I were still friends, but her free time was always spent with Emma now, so it felt more like I'd been demoted to just an acquaintance. She had picked Emma over me, but I wasn't upset anymore. I had a lot going on: I was getting ready for college . . . and I knew life goes on, and friends come and go. It was just like we slowly faded away . . . We didn't have any fights or disagreements or anything . . . Nothing was immediately terrible.

Maddie and I became closer than ever and everything was great. I'd think about Jenny from time to time, especially if something funny or weird happened that I knew would have made her laugh. I still liked her and assumed that she still liked me too.

Moving on. I started MyLifeAsEva on YouTube, and I was going through college. I had new friends from all over and life was pretty good! In fact, one of my best YouTube friends and I were filming an epic video called "How to Make the Cheer/Dance Team!" It was all about giving tips on like projecting the right attitude and look and all that stuff. To come in with a smile. How to behave in the tryouts. How to be nice and respectful to other people. Things I'd wish someone had shown me in a video!

And that's when I got the most random of all random texts.

"Did you see Jenny's subtweet?" this one read.

"Wait, I'm sorry. Jenny? Jenny who? Wait . . . Jenny from high school?"

"Yep! Go look!"

I had been out of touch with her for so long that I literally had to LOOK up Jenny's full name on Twitter and scroll down a long list of girls from all over the world with the same first and last name as hers before I came up on MY Jenny's Twitter. I didn't even know that she HAD a Twitter! As I was scrolling I was thinking, What in the world could this possibly be about? I hadn't even spoken to her in over a year aside from supportive Facebook comments!

And this is what I read, from Jenny on Twitter:

"Why would you make a video called 'How to Make the Cheer/Dance Team' if you aren't even a good dancer?"

"So annoyed, you suck at dancing so what could you even teach people?"

Of COURSE that was about me.

Of all the hater comments and "You're hideously ugly and look like a worm that's been stepped on" comments I've gotten since I started posting regularly on social media, I had never gotten anything like this from a friend before. I had never been so hurt in my life.

I instantly burst into tears. This wasn't some random stranger being critical—that wouldn't have bothered me. They don't know me! No, this was someone I'd really trusted and really loved. Someone that had been a super-important part of my life for years. Sure, she wasn't a part of my life anymore—we'd moved on—but I'd never done anything to hurt her or cause her pain. I was so hurt by the fact that she would be talking crap on Twitter when, first of all, why would you ever stoop that low to subtweet someone who wasn't even in your life anymore; and second of all, she was someone I did nothing wrong to!

Eventually, I dried my tears and started thinking. I was still like, Wow, *why*? Just *why*??? Because it was more out of the blue than Gigi Hadid suddenly dating Zayn.

But then I realized something: People are going to do outrageous things sometimes, and sometimes you're going to be the butt of a really bad day. It's easy to immediately blame ourselves when someone lashes out at us with drama, but PLEASE don't! Most of the time it's NOT your fault.

Maybe Jenny was jealous. I mean, Jenny hadn't exactly had her life turn out as she planned. Her toxic rela-

tionship had ended and she was now dating her high school ex's best friend. I didn't know what was going on in her life, but she didn't seem completely happy on Facebook, and there I was making new friends and filming fun You-Tube videos, and it was pretty obvious that I was in a good place.

Maybe she had just gotten mad for a minute and then felt bad, but couldn't undo it and didn't know how to apologize!

And then I realized it didn't matter why. It mattered that she was capable of doing what she did.

Finally, I realized I had to stop taking something like that personally. I knew better. Whatever Jenny was going through, I felt bad for her. I knew that I wasn't the best dancer on the dance team, even in high school! But I also knew that the video Jenny was making fun of wasn't about how many pirouettes I could do or how high my leg extensions could go. It was about how to be a good person and how to support your team. It was a video solely about empowerment and motivation, and even though Jenny didn't quite understand what my video was about yet, I did.

At first, I wanted to tweet back at her. I wanted to be like, "Actually, Jenny, my video isn't even about dancing skills, you rude piece of caca."

But I didn't. I chose not to succumb to fighting with someone who clearly had her mind in the wrong spot. I knew the satisfaction of not saying anything. I suddenly realized that taking the high road, and continuing to work hard on my video she'd made fun of, was much more rewarding.

Because I knew that the video Meg and I were doing was going to help a lot of people, I stopped feeling hurt. Instead, I just honestly felt really sorry for Jenny. She really let me down.

But she let herself down more.

I can't lie and say I got over this right away. Going through it was hard. I had never dreamed that someone I'd been so close to would turn on me. And I knew that finding a new best friend can take time and energy, because you never know who you're going to click with and learn to trust. And as hard as it is, it's happened to literally everyone I know. Every friend group is going to have disagreements or fights over time. That's just life!

MORE TIPS ON HOW TO SURVIVE A BESTIE BREAKUP

The big question is, How do you find a friend you can trust like I trusted Jenny once upon a time? Because that's what a real, true, genuine friendship is all about. *Trust!*

So how do you know who's real and who's fake? What do you do when you're being lied to and don't know who to trust? I can count on just a couple of fingers how many people I can trust. But you know what? Ultimately, I don't care. I am not hiding anything. I am not afraid to not share *most* of what's going on in my life, because that's what I've always done. Eventually, I can see how many people truly want to be there and how many don't really care. I am trying to get better at recognizing that sometimes people are going through their own stuff and need to bring someone else down to make them feel better—they see a hole in your emotions and just want to make the hole bigger.

 As I just said, caring about people that you can't trust only hurts you!

Life is too short to waste on people who aren't there for you. That doesn't mean you aren't polite or disinterested in someone. Just that your feelings aren't engaged or wasted on someone who can't reciprocate.

 Trust your gut.

If your radar is pinging that something is off, it usually is!

 Be a good friend.

Don't spread gossip. Don't let jealousy undermine who you are as a person.

 Just do your best to push past any lingering hurt.

Don't let things fester, or they can poison you. Once in a while you might see an old photo or hear news of your former besties, and you'll get a little pang for what once was. And then you get other friends. Who have your back.

 And then you move on.

How did I do that? With a trusted squad of my own.

THE SAVAGE SQUAD

Teala and I met three years ago—she's a YouTuber, too—on a shoot. She had already done a bunch of movies, and everyone else at her level was mean to me and thought they were too cool. I assumed I wasn't cool enough to be in her squad and I was kinda scared to meet her. But she was so sweet and so nice and when we started to see each other at different events, I told her that we should hang out sometime, even though I knew that saying that was something that people did all the time without any intention to back it up!

But Teala was different. We did hang out, and she became my best friend in the whole world. She has my back. We can talk about anything. Even our bad hair days. Like our hair in the era of weaves. Or the blond era. Or school. Or boys. Or careers. She is the opposite of Jenny. She has my back. We see each other literally every day when we're in town unless there is a work commitment—we practically live in each other's houses.

But we also wanted more friends to hang out with, so we started recruiting. It sounds kind of funny and weird, but we'd meet someone we liked and we'd go out to dinner to see if we'd all click. It took a while, because we met some girls who seemed shady or boring. And then we met Meredith.

Meredith was another YouTuber, and we went on tour together and I felt she didn't have that many girlfriends, and because we liked her so much we asked if she'd like to be part of our squad. "Yes, I am ready!" she said. "Take me in!"

Next we met Sierra, yet another YouTuber, and we all had the same happy feeling that she was going to be a great friend. And then once, when a boy was texting us and he was thinking we were dumb, I said, "Oh, that's so SAVAGE." We all looked at each other and laughed. "We're the Savage Squad!" I added. We all laughed some more.

Now we have group chats all the time. We talked about everything in our lives—from what we're doing on our travels to what to wear at Coachella to how to make the world a better place to us sitting on the toilet pooping. We send each other goofy photos. We share advice about dating, and tell each other not to do something because it's ridiculous and then we do it anyway and wait for the feedback. Nothing is off-limits. I know how easy it is for group chats to turn you into a shitty person, because one person says something and five others instantly agree and you get off topic and say stupid things and gossip and you can't undo it.

That never happens with the Savage Squad. We inspire each other. We get good ideas and actually act on them. I got to surf with Meredith and she went with me to buy my first board. Meredith and Teala took up boxing and they work out together. We all take dance classes again, and have beach picnics. We're planning charity things to do together.

My Savage Squad has the kind of friends you want to have forever. They restored my faith in who to trust.

HANGING-OUT TIME WITH YOUR OWN SAVAGE SQUAD

You don't need a lot of (or any) money to hang out. Get creative. It's all about doing something that makes you happy.

1 GO MINI GOLFING.
Mini golfing is super inexpensive and a fun way to unwind and laugh with your BFFs.

2 HAVE A PICNIC.
We love buying sandwiches from the grocery store, taking a blanket, and watching the sun set while talking . . . and talking!

3 WATCH A SERIES ON TV OR YOUR COMPUTER.
Teala and I love to scream at the TV while all the characters of *Gossip Girl* do crazy things. It bonds us so close!

4 GET COFFEE.
If we're ever not doing anything, we'll just drive down to the local shopping center, get coffee, and walk around. No buying. Just looking!

For all of us, 2016 was such a crazy year. We let way too many people into our lives—it became this huge web of people so that boys who lived on the smallest island in Hawaii knew someone who knew someone else who was linked to us. Our lives became so complicated and too many people knew each other's business and it got to the point where it was actually scary and we all got stressed out.

One day I made a diagram of all the connections, and when we looked at it, we were shocked. It was so messed up, and we could not believe all the connections we'd just made. We could clearly identify the people in the web who were affecting multiple friendships. Something had to be done.

"What if they're not the problem?" Meredith asked. "What if we are?"

"What do you mean?" I replied.

"Well, what if I never told you about so-and-so and you wouldn't have known who this person was," she explained. "I mean, just because we talk to these people doesn't mean we have to keep talking to them. We need to make our circle smaller."

She was so right. You don't have to like everyone who shows some interest in you. You can be judicious about who you trust. I've learned that the hard way!

So this is our diagram for 2017.

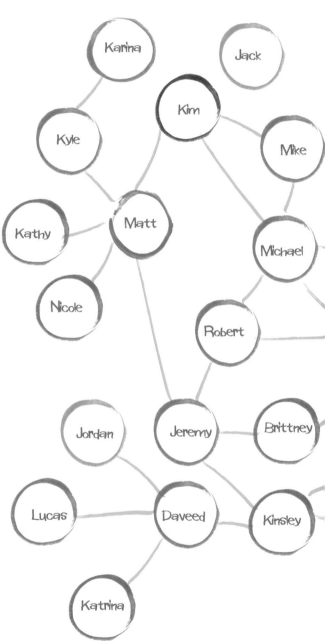

The Four BFFs!

EVA

TEALA

SIERRA

MEREDITH

FOUR WONDERFUL FRIENDS. ONE CIRCLE.
THE SAVAGE SQUAD.

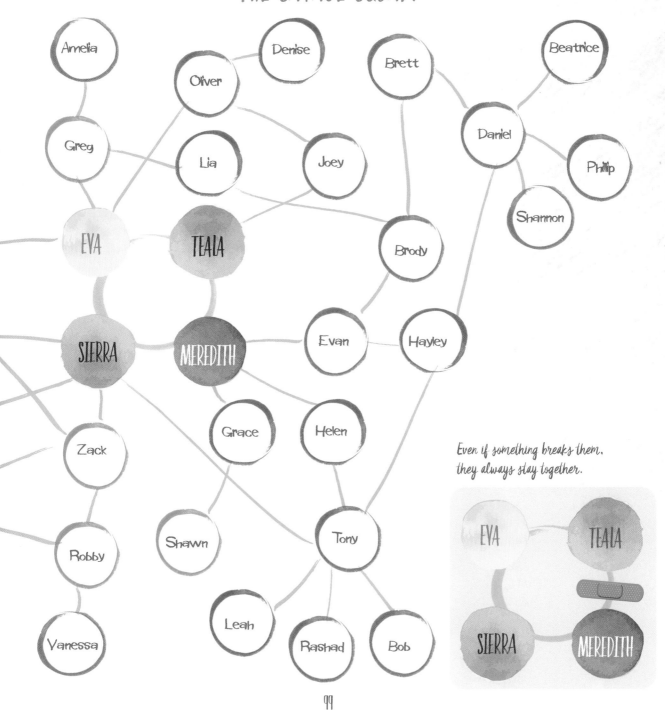

Even if something breaks them,
they always stay together.

BFFS4EVA

CHAPTER 6

BODY IMAGE

G rowing up, I was always the tallest girl in school. I literally sprouted up way ahead of everyone else, and before I knew it, I was eleven years old and looking like my future involved either being a Victoria's Secret model or an Olympic volleyball player. Somehow, I even ended up being the MVP of my community basketball team . . . solely because I could see above everyone else's heads.

That was the only reason. I sucked at basketball otherwise!

I was incredibly strong too. In junior high, my school had to do physical fitness testing every October, and I would always make it my goal to set the record for the most push-ups and pull-ups in the grade. I beat all the girls by a landslide,

and even beat the boys' numbers. I made sure to show off to them, and I'm pretty sure I told the entire school that I did sixty-seven sit-ups and Kyle Matthews only did sixty-two.

Sports were something I liked to show off about. I absolutely killed it in sports, and was better than most of the boys in my school—and not just in fitness testing. I loved proving to boys that I was really good at something they too could be good at, so at lunch, I was always kicking around a soccer ball and joining in on their field football games. I didn't ever want anyone to tell me I was pretty or cool—I just wanted everyone to be wowed by the things I could do, because I really was pretty good at them.

I tried out for the school track team, and found out that I was one of the best high jumpers around. It was the most fun thing ever, and I was loving life because I beat pretty much all my competition with ease. I guess maybe I realized that I wasn't "hot" like a lot of the other girls my age, so I couldn't really follow that route . . . but when you're good at sports, everyone likes you.

It felt cool to have something different going for me. I was always the tomboy, badass athlete girl that would be ruthlessly slide-tackling people left and right for the ball. I felt like I had something special.

Then I got to high school.

You see, it turned out that while I was tall, thin, and pretty good at sports my whole life, when I got to high school my height was just average. My body wasn't special or unique, and nearly everyone was better at sports than me. Things about me that I had found unique weren't unique anymore. I was just another five-foot-four girl with a size seven-and-a-half shoe, and every time I went shoe shopping, size seven-and-a-half would be the only size they didn't have, which constantly reminded me that I fell into the most average category of person, even down to my feet.

Suddenly, and unexpectedly, I was lost. Who was I? No longer could I keep up with such amazing, better, more serious athletes from other schools. No

longer could I spring from bed every morning, look at myself in the mirror, and say, "Wow, Eva, you're so tall and strong!" For a while, I didn't know what was special about me anymore. It took me quite a bit of time, but then I realized something: Everyone has special qualities about themselves. EVERYONE! Even if you don't think so sometimes, or haven't found it yet, guess what? You are the BEST at *something*. Better than anyone else. Just being you, a combination of many things, is enough to be the best at.

Look at me! I still have goofy teeth that show way too much of my gums. I have chipped toenail polish 99 percent of the time. I don't have big boobs, but I can still feel like a Victoria's Secret model on the inside. My under-eye highlight is almost always too strong (blend, Eva, *blend*!), but I look damn cute when I tap a non-dynamic, two-fingered performance of Bill Withers's "Lean on Me" on the piano for my friends.

That's my look! Those are some little, funny things I happen to be really good at rocking. Along with being able to beat nearly anyone in my school in a race, and secretly taking really good photos of people, and showing off how awesome my ninja kick is to people all the time . . . too often—even though I've never taken kickboxing.

WHAT ARE SOME OF THE LITTLE, FUNNY THINGS YOU'RE PRETTY GOOD AT??

1.
2.
3.
4.
5.
6.
7.
8.
9.
10.
11.
12.
13.
14.

We can all get caught up in our-selves when somebody else suddenly turns out to be even better at something we think we were good at. It's almost impossible not to make comparisons. It's like when you really want that latest pair of Nikes, and when you finally get them, you strut around in front of your mirror, modeling them back to yourself, taking those hot mirror pics because you feel ABSOLUTELY amazing in them. You feel like a straight 100. Then, the next day, you're flicking through the pages of a magazine and you see Kendall Jenner wearing them . . . with a much cuter out-fit then you own . . . and you're instantly deflated. You know you don't look like that. And you don't feel like a 100 any-more, but more like a 30, lost in a world of 40s, 60s, and the occasional shiny 100. But if you lined up a skinny supermodel, a plus-size girl, a boy, and YOU, all wear-ing the same outfit, and asked someone to pick who looks the best, who's to say that they wouldn't pick you? Everyone has different ideas about what they like; there's something for everyone. Espe-cially YOU.

The idea that there will always be someone better than you because they "look" better appearance-wise, or perform better at something needs to change. If you get up into the line and are absolutely working it, posing, smil-ing, and feeling yourself, you can shine through anyone else.

I realized that if we all get caught up in trying to be the hottest and best athlete or dancer or whatever on the planet, we'd literally go insane. Don't push to be the best and get constantly beat down when people keep passing you. Push to have fun, push to smile, and push to rock what you've got. Laugh at yourself when you fail, and learn from those who pass you in your favorite talent instead of hating them!

For example, I loved soccer, and I thought it would be my life. But then tons of girls got better at all the skills than me, and for a really long time, I stopped play-ing. How could I play and feel so embar-rassed if I was the worst out of the team? Then I realized I had to just keep playing. Playing soccer was always all about fun for me, not about needing to win or being the best. So I played with the girls who were better than me. I didn't flinch when the coaches were always telling me to look at what so-and-so does when she passes because it's the best. I had longer nights on the field trying to get skills right, and I took tons and tons of advice from the better soccer players. And I im-proved more than I ever thought I could.

So, big deal, I never went to college on a soccer scholarship, which is what I thought I would do when I was twelve, but that's okay. I knew that being a professional soccer player was not one of my life goals. But that doesn't stop me from fully enjoying the game. To this day I still own three soccer balls that are always in the back of my car. I love to challenge people to a game, even though my stamina is weak and I want to pass out after ten minutes of playing. I still get absolutely schooled by people better than me, but being the best doesn't matter to me anymore. All that matters is me having fun doing things I love.

PUT A BIG X ON THE COMPARISONS AND COMMENTING, AND LEARN TO LOVE YOUR BODY

Social media can be an amazing place to meet people just like you and find what inspires you! But with all the amazing things that it brings, it can also bring some negatives. One of the big problems with social media is how easy it is to hide behind a fake username and make comments about somebody. And this is a real problem when you're talking about body image.

Back when I was in high school, Instagram was NOT a thing. Can you believe that? No Kylie Jenner. No Flashback Friday. No Facetune and no filters. Nobody cared! Obviously, body image issues are not a new idea. They've been going on since humans were put on this planet, but

as the years have gone by, body image instigators have gone from seeing a drawing of a pretty girl in a newspaper ad to a way more complicated world of ads, commercials, real-life moments, music videos, Instagram Photoshoppers, and more. It's overwhelming, and it makes it a LOT harder to love yourself in this modern day.

Whether you're a size AA or DD, or a size zero or a size twenty-two, you need to love your body. It can be so hard when your body is changing to love your own skin and feel comfortable in it. Especially if you're losing or gaining weight, or you took birth control pills to make your period better and suddenly you're three sizes bigger and have huge boobs. Your body is going to do some crazy stuff during puberty, and just when you think you're comfortable with yourself, your body will flip-flop and take a new form in a matter of months. It's all about changing and learning to adapt and love the way your body grows and changes. It's also important to know that everyone's body changes differently.

For example, my sister and I have very different bodies. It's just the way we're built. I'm small and skinny like my mom—actually, she's even skinnier than me. My sister is more like my grandmother, with more curves. Growing up, I faced the problem where I was wondering, "Hey nature . . . ha-ha, um, when are my boobs coming in? Is that on your to-do list? Oh, it's not? Oh, okay, thanks." I was always wondering when my curves would happen and I would turn into a "woman," whereas my sister grew up skinny and then all of a sudden her body was like, "Hey girl, I'm going to give you so many curves you're going to look like what happened when Pepsi decided to reshape their bottle in 2013." Her body went through more dramatic changes than mine did, mainly because mine didn't want to change at all. We are just different!

Plus, I eat more than all the friends I've ever had. When I go to restaurants, you can ask any of my friends and they'll tell you that I order two meals. I easily can eat five full meals a day and still be hungry. I am just one of those people with a super-high metabolism. I am active, I love sports, I love food, I love to eat, and I love feeling good and taking care of myself. Yet for some reason, people who don't know me think that because of my body type I must be "starving myself" or "unhealthy!" To call someone out with serious accusations like "anorexic" or "obese" because of how they look on the outside is not funny one bit. It's what causes people to go crazy and obsess over how they look when they shouldn't! Anyone calling someone names of

disorders that you don't even know anything about can actually cause the perfectly happy person to start having body image issues. People are quick to judge you on your body type because they are confused by it. They only truly know their own body, and since everyone's body is different, they don't understand how yours works. You may be the picture of health and have a gorgeous curvy body that you feel great in, and some hater is still going to call you "fat" and try to convince you that you should look like them.

The perfect body isn't even real. It's like when people ask you, "Who is the perfect human?" Well, some people may answer, "Blue eyes, brown hair, five foot three," when someone else might say, "Brown eyes, tan skin, six feet with freckles." There is absolutely no way the whole world or even three people in the same room have the same combination of things they love about a person's size and shape.

We need to stop worrying about impressing others and just think about impressing ourselves every new day. Ask yourself what makes YOU feel good. Not what makes the *world* feel good. If you woke up every day trying to be perfect so the world liked you, you'd go absolutely bonkers.

The other day I was with my British YouTube guy friends and we were shopping for shoes. I saw a pair of Nikes in a cool color, and instantly remembered seeing tons of hot girls wearing the same Nikes all over Tumblr and Instagram. The girls all wore tight athletic wear and had perfect long hair with perfect gleaming highlights, and those clean stylish Nike shoes. I figured maybe I could be hot too like them, if I got the shoes, got the tight leggings, and posed like the girls had done. So I asked the boys for their opinion.

"Hey, what's your favorite style on a girl?" I said them, ever so casually. "Do you like girls that wear track shoes and, like, Adidas and Nike and leggings and all of that?"

You know what they said?

One by one, they all answered, "I just look at their face, not their clothes."

I was like, Are you serious???? Tell me you're not just being nice to me by saying that. Surely you have to like a certain style on a girl!

They just explained to me that if a girl has a nice smile and can be confident and make them laugh, they didn't care what she was wearing or what her body looked like!

Whoa. That opened my eyes so much!

I was so focused on buying all the clothes the girls I saw on Tumblr wore because I thought it would get me closer to making people like me! And then I real-

ized it's not the outfits you wear or the hairstyle you do that matters. It's who's rocking the look—and that's you.

Sure, there will always be a lot of guys that *do* look at what you're wearing, and *do* feel they have the right to judge you based on your weight or your shape, and *do* make snarky comments—but those will never be the guys you want to talk to!

So don't be too hard on yourself. I think it's really important to get good eating and exercise habits in place when you're in high school—but that's because you need to take care of your health, not because you need to look a certain way. Feeling good about your body isn't about starving yourself into thinness. It's about being a healthy weight that is the right weight for you. It's about having strong muscles. It's about taking care of your skin.

And it's about realizing that nearly everybody else is probably struggling with their own body image too.

WHAT TO DO WHEN YOU'RE HAVING ISSUES WITH YOUR WEIGHT

There are several things I recommend:

 Get a comprehensive checkup.

Don't be in denial like I've been (oops!), and see a doctor

for a full checkup to make sure you are healthy. You will read more about this in the "Health" chapter, but yes, you need to do this even when you're a teenager! I know of kids whose thyroids were way out of whack and they started gaining weight and were being super tired all the time—and it wasn't their fault. I also know of other kids who suddenly lost tons of weight and were crazy thirsty all the time—they had diabetes, which is really serious and can actually kill you if it's not brought under control. (I know this because my grandpa has diabetes.) You'll never get your weight where you want it to be if there's an underlying medical issue you aren't aware of.

2 **Be fully aware of what you're eating AND drinking.**

Do you know how many calories are in those jumbo lattes or smoothies you drink every day? It's actually scary . . . because it's enough for breakfast and lunch. Even healthy green drinks can secretly (and often) end up being bad for you! Be sure you know what you're putting into your body, whether it's solid or liquid. I used to make fun of those moms who would read the labels at the grocery store, but they're actually being smart about calorie counts and stuff you don't want to eat—like hidden sugar and fat.

3 **Turn on the stove!**

The best way to watch what you eat and drink is by doing your own cooking. You can control the amount of ingredients you're using, and you can use fresh food that is so much better for you than anything that's packaged and processed.

I'm really glad my mom and grandma taught me the basics, because cooking is such an important skill to have. Which, I have to admit, I *don't* always have! Especially the time I tried to microwave a container of Cup Noodles with no water in it . . . and it set off so many sparks and then exploded and set the microwave on fire. Not a good look!

When I cook, I like to make basics, especially if they're in one pot. They're easy to make and a whole lot easier to clean up. I love Mexican food, especially tacos and burritos. It helps to make a big batch and then freeze the leftovers too.

THE BEST WAY TO KEEP YOUR WEIGHT AT A HEALTHY PLACE IS TO MOVE IT MOVE IT MOVE IT!

You already know how important it is to get a move on, of course! Exercise burns calories while you're doing it. It gives you strong muscles that rev up your metabolism even more. It improves your circulation and your breathing. It helps regulate your appetite. Even more important—it makes you feel really good.

You already know what a super-active girl I was and still am. I was so lucky to have grown up in Southern California, where the weather is made for being outside most of the time. I was on a boys' soccer team when I was three. I owned my first skateboard by twelve, and was a shark-level swimmer at the local community pool by thirteen.

Okay, "shark level" actually just meant I was able to dive for rings and not die. But anyways.

Even though I was strong enough to beat the boys at sit-ups in elementary school, I never was thrilled with the actual gym classes, although I picked up sports pretty well. It just wasn't me. I got anxiety. Once I got older, a lot of my friends started going to different gyms for their workouts. I tried to go with them but would always feel so uncomfortable. I'm not a "gym" person. I just always feel really out of place and self-conscious in a gym, like everyone's staring at me, even if there's only one or two other people in there—and they're busy doing their own workouts.

Because I was never a gym person, it sucks, because I feel like now, when people are told they need to lose weight, they're made to believe their only option

is to go to the dreaded GYM. But the gym can be scary, trainers are ridiculously expensive, and it takes time to get there and then get back home. If I were having weight or health concerns and the only way to fix them meant I had to go to the gym, I'd be in bad shape, because there's NO way you can get me in a gym.

So how do I stay in shape? I love running, especially on a track where I can alternate a jogging pace with sprinting. I still like to play soccer with my friends, as you know, especially on the beach. I go kayaking with my BFFs, which is a blast. I love skateboarding, which needs a lot of balancing skill, so that engages your core muscles and keeps my belly flat.

And I love, love, love surfing. Not just because the surfers are so hot—talk about a great workout! Especially for my upper body and core.

Have you noticed a common theme? The kind of exercise I like to do is *fun*. It takes place outdoors. It doesn't feel like a chore—which is how I feel about getting down to do a set of crunches. That's so boring—it's actually agonizing to me. In other words, how I exercise is always about taking the work out of working out.

Speaking of fun . . .

Getting Yourself into the Workout Groove

1 Give dance a try.

Really. It doesn't matter what kind you do—dancing is the best!

I've been dancing nearly all my life—ballet, tap, jazz, you name it—and I can't imagine ever not dancing! I absolutely love to dance. As soon as the music comes on, I'm in another world.

Dancing is also one of the best ways to lose weight. My sister was worried about gaining weight, and as soon as she started regular classes, off came the pounds. Even if you think you're not coordinated, you can dance. It just takes practice. Everyone can improve, and everyone will have fun!

Not only that, but dance is really good at helping you improve your mental coordination too. You have to focus on learning and repetition all the time—but it doesn't feel like work, because you're not sitting in a classroom. You're moving to music. The music propels you. It makes it so much easier to get up and do it, and the time just flies by.

If you've never danced before, there's no better time to start than right now. See if there's a beginners' class in your community. Look for a class like Zumba, which is geared to newbies and is a ton of fun. Or go on YouTube. There are a gazillion videos with incredible teachers and music, and you can practice at your own speed in the privacy of your home until you get your confidence up. I know you can do it!

I really, really hope you will try a dance class. Yes, I stopped playing soccer in high school when I was beating myself up about not being good enough and then started it up again because I still loved the game and really liked being on the team, but you're always running this way and that way, and that's all that's on your mind. Kicking the ball and scoring and running.

But dance? It's not stationary, of course, but you aren't traveling the way you do in soccer. You're in a rehearsal room or on a stage, and your only "goal" is to learn the steps and then perfect them.

Even better is that you're not doing it alone. I realized this when I was trying so hard to be on the dance team. For me, I need a group, or to be on a team. I get my motivation from being around other people. It's really satisfying to be part of a team, even if I'm on the bench most of the time! Because you're in it together.

So while there's probably going to be drama and egos and all that, you're all focused on a common goal. You're going to have to figure out the best way to get along, and doing that is often a lot better than winning all the time!

Whatever kind of exercise you choose to do, have it be your passion.

Some people like cerebral kinds of sports like tennis or volleyball. Others really thrive on solitary workouts like running or cycling. They like to be alone with their thoughts or their music, and that suits their personalities. Ask me to go on a hike up and down a mountain—forget about it!

I learned my lesson about that when I was in Hawaii last year. I can go to dance classes and rehearse for hours and hours, but ask me to do a strenuous activity like hiking up hills, and I'm suddenly way too busy. Okay, I can do a long hike as long as it's not seven miles and the company is good, just so you know!

MY TWO FAVORITE RECIPES

yum

MY GRANDPA'S CHICKEN SOUP

I don't eat chicken anymore, so you can take out the chicken if you don't eat meat as well, but my grandpa's soup was a staple in my house. My family was often on the go, always struggling to keep up with having me and my sister in school and trying to just make enough to support our family and put $3 of gas in the tank. Food to our family was often quick and easy, like boiling some noodles and sauce for pasta late at night and eating it on the couch while watching whatever my grandpa wanted to watch. Every so often, however, my grandpa would return home from the grocery store with bags full of celery, carrots, noodles, rice, a chicken, and more. My grandma would get out this giant soup pot that was about two feet tall, and I would know the soup was coming and life was okay again. Grandpa would only make this two or three times a year. Maybe even less frequently. I remember it was special. It took two days to make, and when it was done we would eat it for three days straight until it all ran out. This soup was everything.

INGREDIENTS

1 bunch carrots
4 stalks celery
3 onions
1 bunch parsley
1 whole chicken
Salt and pepper

Cut the veggies into chunks, and the parsley into small pieces and put into a pot. Add the chicken. Add water until the chicken is fully submerged. Heat up to a low boil and cook it for a few hours until the chicken falls apart. Stir occasionally. Add salt and pepper to taste. The best way to make soup is to let everything really cook for a long time, then enjoy it with your family. Soup is meant to be shared!

VEGAN CHILI

In February 2016, I stopped eating meat. This was one of the best decisions of my life. I loved getting inspired with new ways to eat to stay healthy with different kinds of protein, and started trying so many new foods. One of the things I learned to make is some bomb chili. I always thought, What's chili without some meat? until I made it without meat or cheese and was literally mind-blown. This is great to make when you're having friends over who are vegetarian and/or vegan. Then you don't have to worry about them not eating what you cooked! Also, you don't need exact measurements—just use more or fewer beans depending on how large a batch you want to make.

INGREDIENTS

1-2 cans black beans
1-2 cans red beans
Spicy chili sauce
1-2 stalks celery, chopped
1 can corn
Cumin
Garlic powder
Paprika

Heat up the black beans, red beans, and corn. Add the spicy chili sauce and heat up to a simmer. While this is cooking, chop the celery, then add and stir until the celery has softened just a bit and has gotten hot. Add in a dash of cumin, a dash of garlic powder, and a dash of paprika. I love about six or seven dashes of each to make it extra flavorful, but that's just me! Enjoy your amazing vegan chili!

yum

JUNIOR

EVA'S NEWS

CHAPTER 7

Glo—Up Level, JUNIOR STYLE

Junior year was when I decided to be a broadcast journalist. I was obsessed with Oprah and Katie Couric at the time. Seems crazy, I know!

So I thought, Okay, if I want this career I have to start dressing the part. I cut my hair so it was a shorter and more flippy journalist style. For back-to-school shopping I went and purchased what I thought were proper interviewer clothes. Dark-wash skinny jeans and button-down shirts with bow ties that would look good on the morning news, and new boots with heels. Brown boots with buckles on the side. I was the literally the only person in my school wearing boots like that.

This was also the year I became friends with all the seniors because I was dating a senior. They were all doing the whole hoodie-and-Abercrombie look. OMG my clothes were so ugly!

I didn't care. I LOVED them. I was so obsessed with these boots, because they made me taller, and as I walked, they went *click-clack* on the ground and I felt like such a badass me every day! I especially felt like this new person and so much older and was totally feeling myself with my adult look.

But then, by the end of the year, I realized it wasn't me. That was the first time I had a phone with a camera. It was a really crappy camera, but no prob—it worked! I was taking photos and experimenting with different angles and things and I started to look all hot and sexy and older, and my dad was starting to freak. My parents wouldn't let me shop at Forever 21 because my dad said older ladies who want to actually *be* forever twenty-one dressed like twenty-one-year-olds and I wasn't twenty-one so I couldn't go there. He was so off! I got mad, but then I figured it out. Because I found so much great Forever 21 stuff when thrifting. And my dad never looked at the labels. They cost a tenth of the price, and I could afford tons more outfits. Ka-ching!

This was also the first time I got a push-up bra. And my hair was growing out and was getting more sleek and shiny. Even my poop ponytail was better. Especially for prom. My mom did my makeup that year, and I looked really good.

With this growing confidence, I realized I should stop looking like a newscaster and look my own age.

So I did.

STYLE

CHAPTER 8

STYLING

It can be SO easy to stop caring about your own unique style thing when you have so many other things to focus on. And you can tell from my glo-ups that I sometimes was too much of a fashion follower, rather than a fashion forwarder. Looking back, most of the people at my school that I thought were dressing cool and all-American were just looking like boring clones of each other. When I think about who really stood out with their style, it was girls who were taking risks, wearing unique pieces, and adding color into their wardrobes. Girls with the coolest style weren't just looking like pages out of *Vogue* magazine. They came in all types of styles, like punk or goth or hippie. They made it seem so easy, and I really envied them. They totally did not care what anyone thought of their outfits, because they were dressing for themselves, not to please anybody else. And that's what actually makes someone cool.

It's so important to remember to showcase who you are, even when you're busy writing essays and finishing math assignments while trying not to bash your calculator to bits with a shovel. When we get lost in how much "stuff' we have to get done, we forget, hey, wait a second, we're also human beings that are supposed to have some fun and smile and learn about ourselves!

Style helps us recognize who WE are while we're busy doing work for someone ELSE. So even though the last thing on your mind while you're rushing to finish homework is being "unique," remember that it's still very important. I mean, seriously, homework sucks, but what sucks more is graduating from high school and realizing you played it too safe and never failed hard enough to get these awesome throwback pictures to look back on!

HOW TO FIND YOUR OWN STYLE

My style has gone through so many crazy phases. From band tees and rattails to the thrift store version of Blair Waldorf, I've had a lot of moments to look back on. Though my style is always changing, it's important to realize every time I changed styles, it was because I was inspired. A lot of times it was inspiration from a character in a book I read or a movie I saw. But it wasn't just because I loved their style. It was what their style said about *them* that I wanted to say about *me* as well.

To find your style, look all around you for inspiration. See what colors you love, what fabrics you think are always cool, what feelings you get when you see an outfit you love—and then go hunting for pieces that fit all of your inspirations! You can't just go into a store without knowing at least a little bit of what you're looking for and what you personally have been dying to try on. Stores give me major anxiety, with all the lights and music and people, so whenever I go shopping, I clearly have in my head, "Oh, I remember that pair of blue denim flare jeans Gigi Hadid wore in London last week and I'd love to find something in a similar style," or, "OMG how cool would it be to find something velvet in a color I love, because I freaking LOVE velvet." I always go in with a little wish list that I hope I find, and if I find an item on that list, then I've succeeded!

But style doesn't have to be found in a mall or while online shopping. Growing up, I got a lot of my style straight from the thrift shop. And not trendy vintage thrift shops. I'm talking Salvation Army, baby-toys-in-the-corner, old-microwave-and-lamp-collection-in-the-back thrift shop. You would never in a million years think someone could come out of that store with style. But I did! Every chance I could get to go, I would stock up on $20 worth of finds, which was a LOT. I found things that no one else was wearing in school, and I looked super unique!

In order to afford to keep thrift shopping, I had to make some money. One way my friends and I made money was to have "closet sales" on Facebook. We'd take photos of all our clothes we wanted to get rid of, and add comments and a price (like a couple of dollars), and my grandma would drive me around to all the buyers in the neighborhood. My favorite captions were "Crop top from some store in LA—$4," and "Forever 21 Greek pretty dress that makes people's boobs look good—$5." Once other girls from the school caught on, it became a major thing, and suddenly girls at school that couldn't afford to go shopping all the time were trading, tipping, and giving clothes to one another. It became a community sisterhood shopping center, all on our Facebook pages.

Now that's what I call *stylin'*.

NOW PUT YOUR STYLE TO WORK IN YOUR BEDROOM OR APARTMENT

If you've seen my YouTube videos, you have a pretty good idea of what my apartment looks like. I love my Christmas lights, my bed pillows, and all my little knickknacks floating around. I have a tapestry above my computer and a dream catcher, as well as some DIY projects I love. I'd say my room is pretty dang Tumblr blog–approved.

But sometimes, every so often, I'll see someone make a comment like, "This could be my room but I don't have any money," or, "This is a room only for rich people," which make me really sad, because, in fact, everything in my room is not only cheap, but able to be made on a dime! When people make these sort of comments, it reminds me of when I was in high school, thinking nothing could be done without maybe some more time or maybe some more money. Since I was little, I've always done the little things I could do make my room look good, and even though today my room is a little cleaner with some newer things, it's still the same approach! Here's a list of my favorite things in my bedroom and how you too can make them:

1 Christmas lights

Buy them in January, right after the holidays. They'll be super cheap and they last so long. Those fairy lights on the gold wires are cool, but Christmas lights shine way brighter, and you get more for your money. Just make sure to get the white lights on white cord, so they blend in nicely with anything and give a great glow effect. Then take them home and hang them all over with some clear pushpins. Boom! You can make any space look alive and cute with some lights.

2 Cute pillows

Pillows and bedding make or break a room. I am a big fan of collecting warm blankets that feel like cinnamon rolls wrapped around my body, but I also love making my bed look like a Pottery Barn ad even if nothing's from that store! So whenever I shop for warm blankets, I always make sure to get them in a neutral color like white, cream, or black, just so it goes with all the fun stuff in my room like funky pillows and tapestries. For pillows and bedding, I just make my own. It's easy to make a pillow cover and comforter, and you can even make them both out of just fabric and hot glue. Then, you decide your pattern. Go to a fabric store, get a few yards of inexpensive fabric, and make some pillow covers—they're a great way to instantly change the look of your room.

3 Knickknacks

I may have golden pig book-ends, Polaroid cameras, and anthropology books now, but years ago I had the same things, just from different places. Head into the decor aisle of the thrift store, as you might be surprised at what you find. They have the CUTEST serving plates ever, which you can use to put jewelry or perfumes on. They have vintage cameras, books that are only a few cents, and so many cool picture frames and candles. I stock up on little decor pieces there all the time and fill my room with them.

4 Tapestries and wall art

People like to charge you $40 for what they call a "tapes-try" or a "vintage print," but in reality, you can make these both yourself. Go to the fabric store, get two yards of cool patterned fabric, and tack it to your wall. Boom. Tapestry. Go to the print store and ask them to print you an 8" x 11" of this quote you saw on Tumblr. Hang it to your wall. Boom. Trendy wall art.

It's so easy to make your room have style! Don't be discouraged if you can't get your hands on something, especially if it's pricey. Just make it happen yourself!

SOCIAL

The FOUR STAGES

YOU READ SOMETHING,

YOU LET IT HIT YOU,

# of ONLINE BULLYING

THEN YOU REALIZE YOUR **WORTH** and HOW COOL YOU REALLY ARE, FLAWS and ALL.

SLAY *the* HATERS!

CHAPTER 9

BULLYING

emember the burn book in the movie *Mean Girls*? Something so terrible that it could only ever exist in movies or books . . . right? Well, that's what I thought too until one day, at the end of sophomore year, a folded-up piece of white paper was slipped onto my desk. I quickly opened it.

"SENIOR SECONDS," I read.

What was this "Senior Seconds?" I asked the kid next to me, who appeared to be the one who had slid it onto my desk, because he was eyeing me like the side-eye smirking emoji.

"It's only the coolest list E-VER," he replied; then he leaned in close, as if he were filling me in on some ancient Halloween ghost story. "Every year, on the last week of high school, someone will put out a list . . . the Seeeeenior Sec-ondsssss," he went on. "The list has ALL the hottest dirt on anyone who's ANY-ONE in school. It. Exposes. Everything."

I looked at the piece of paper again and saw that it was kind of like a list of names with little blurbs next to every one of them. It was well thought-out. It was a typed, organized document. I recognized some of the names on the paper—hot senior dance team girls that I looked up to. Then I realized that this piece of paper was really freaking mean.

I was shocked! Basically, Senior Seconds was a list that someone started to make fun of how, in yearbooks, people are nominated for things like "Most Likely to Succeed!" and "Prettiest Smile!"— only this was the dark, messed-up version of that. Typically, the list was small, so only the most popular of the popular kids made it on. I joked about how I had nothing to worry about, because I would never in a million years make it onto one of those stupid lists.

Fast-forward to my junior year. I had a big year—so much better than the previous one! I made friends with lots of the senior squad and even dated one of their most cherished own, but I was just a junior, so when it was time for the Senior Seconds list to inevitably be released, the last thing I expected was for my name to make it on.

I remember this so clearly. June 13 came along, and it was second period. Talk of the Senior Seconds list was buzzing around, and that it had been dropped in a bathroom during passing period. Naturally, everyone was trying to get their hands on it. Typically, the tradition went that whoever stepped forth to make the terrible list would print out a few copies and hide them around school, and the contents would be spread by word of mouth, or if someone was brave

enough, they'd surreptitiously xerox the list using a copy machine.

Well, this year was different. Kids at school started getting nicer phones, and they realized that they could take pictures of the list and send it to their friends. This was the first time the Senior Seconds list—and mass bullying in my school— became a big thing. Suddenly, anyone with a phone that could receive picture messages and any vague connection to a senior kid with some social status could read the list. Freshmen that didn't know anyone who was even on the list could have drama to discuss that they actually knew nothing about!

And when the list finally got around to me, I realized that I WAS ON IT.

"JC: Most likely to get a scholarship for college basketball and be benched the entire year," read one of the comments. "PS, your little junior girlfriend was cute. I wonder how screwing her worked."

I rolled my eyes. Here we went again! I never had sex with JC, but the world wanted to believe that we did, because he was seven feet tall and I had never gotten any taller than my five foot four. Everyone wanted so badly to make jokes on our height differences.

I just brushed it off, because me being on the Senior Seconds list ended up just being a stupid remark on my relationship, and nothing that was actually true. My friends tried to cheer me up by saying that I should look at the bright side—that only the most popular kids in school were put on Senior Seconds, and wasn't I glad that I was so popular? Uh, no, I was not! Not if it meant that I'd be bullied like that. It didn't bother me too much, but for other people, the bully who wrote it took it way too far.

Unfortunately, we all know that most schools are pretty clueless when it comes to knowing what to do about bullying, but my school decided that if you were caught being responsible for writing that horrible list, you would be banned from walking at graduation. It sounded scary, but the school never really went to any great lengths to figure out who wrote it, and no one ever really ended up getting in trouble for it.

Anyway, the year after I graduated, the Senior Seconds list got even worse, because the bullies who created it decided to go digital. The list didn't show up in the bathrooms anymore, and it wasn't printed on paper—it was only put up on a Facebook page that you could Like and add as a friend! The Senior Seconds list makers put out horrible facts and bullying comments about people in the form of status updates that

everyone could see, and even thumbs-up if they dared to.

Did Facebook shut it down? No, they did not. And you know why?

Because no one complained to them.

So the bullies had the last laugh. Total strangers who were told about it could ask to get on the page, and more people than ever could see the Senior Seconds list. It wasn't just seniors and a few "lucky" juniors. It was everyone—even kids from other schools, and potential future colleges or employers that the people on the list would be attending or applying to. It became much more detrimental. To this day, I can still look up the Senior Seconds list and find all of the terrible things they said about kids who went to my school.

I don't know if the Senior Seconds list still exists at my old high school, but after I graduated, I ran into some terrible Twitter pages and Instagram pages that were used for the same thing—only not just at the end of the year. A fully running social media world was going on just to make fun of and spill drama about kids at my school. It was absolutely terrible.

Cyberbullying is so much worse than face-to-face bullying. It enables anyone to create a fake account and post whatever they want, without fears of an immediate in-their-face reaction. It makes normally nice people say things online that they would never dream of saying out loud.

And it is not going to stop, either.

Unless we work together to make people realize it's going to do nothing but hurt everyone in the end, even the bully! There are people I know that used to bully kids in high school and online, and they still can't even forgive themselves for what they mindlessly wrote about people. It's absolutely disgusting!

It's way too easy to get caught up in a delusional world where you pass off saying horrible things about someone as having "freedom of speech" and just "stating your opinion." But it's important to know that opinions are different than talking behind someone's back ruthlessly. Online, talking behind someone's back is like tweeting a subtweet. You're not mature enough to let someone live their life, so you have to comment about it so you still think you're brave by being "public," while in reality you really hope only your closest friends see it and think you're "funny." Posting subtweets, indirects, and even direct comments on someone's page—claiming to just be "stating an opinion"—is actually often bullying.

How would you like it if you posted an Instagram selfie of you looking relaxed and confident on the beach, just trying to build a sand castle with your family, and twenty kids from your school commented things like "Fat," "She's gained weight so she should honestly eat a salad . . . just my opinion," or even commented using pig emojis and laughing emojis? How would you feel? It's just so NOT okay. Comments like these that have no purpose except to hurt are forms of bullying.

Now, imagine that these twenty kids turned into two thousand kids. That's what I have to deal with every day!

So how do you protect yourself from cyberbullies?

I ask myself this question all the time.

The immediate and disappointing answer is, you can't. Bullies will be bullies, and their line of thinking often stems from a sad train line of one person getting hated on, and then they think, Well, if I'm getting hated on, then whatever, I'm going to go hate on some people too, so they know how it feels! But whatever you do, you CAN'T get caught up in that terrible train line. You have to be the person that stops the train dead on its tracks and rids the area of bullies. And if we have more people stopping this train of bullies, then the bullies eventually have nowhere else to go. They will be forced to get off the train and walk on home.

I wish I could be more positive about this, but the only way you can protect yourself from being cyberbullied is to have no social media profile at all, which isn't realistic, because social media is now how we communicate with each other. So there really is no protection. Twitter has to be practically slammed by thousands and thousands of complaints before they remove someone. Facebook isn't much better.

So you can't protect yourself from getting cyberbullied. It's going to happen, because there are simply too many people who didn't have someone brave enough to stop the train, and too many people are still thinking it's okay to bully.

What you can do, however, is choose to know that your worth is far stronger than a bully's false words and pathetic comments.

Believe me, if I let everything people said about me knock me down, I wouldn't be alive now. I get horrible comments on the daily from people who think they know me!

Not long ago, for instance, I found myself on a big Instagram page that claimed to be an account "exposing celebrities." I laughed and wondered what could possibly be "exposed" about me. And then I saw that it was a collage photo—one photo from a year ago was lined up next to a photo from a month

ago. What did the person who put the photos up write? "EVA'S LIP INJECTIONS EXPOSED. SHE THINKS SHE FOOLED US, SHE'S SO DUMB."

At first glance, I was furious! Because the photo they used on the "before" side was a photo of me laughing and smiling, and if any real friend or fan saw that, they'd know that I have a smile that makes my lips curl in, and 90 percent of my gums show up to my brain. I've always had a smile like that! The second photo was me trying desperately to look like a Kardashian, with a fresh coat of pink lipstick on, doing a duck face. OF COURSE my lips were going to look different—I was doing two dramatically different expressions!

After that photo went up, the comments quickly piled up: "Yeah, yeah, she definitely got lip injections." Followed by similar comments: "She definitely got lip injections. I can tell!" And there I was, reading hundreds of people discussing whether or not I got lip injections, when I knew that I hadn't gotten lip injections—and that the whole topic was ridiculous.

And you know the worst thing about it? If I had jumped into the conversation and said, "Hey, it's me, Eva, and I did NOT get lip injections and I never will!" no one would have believed me. They wanted to believe the gossip.

It's examples like this that make you realize that out of all the people in the world, an awfully high percentage of them are downright crazy. They're bullies. They're not hiding it. They're not being coy about it. They honestly don't care. And that's the most pathetic thing of all.

I'd like to believe that there are still a lot of people who can realize that they don't have to jump on the bandwagon or agree with something they don't know anything about just because someone else said it. Some people just get influenced really quickly or are jealous or had a bad day and they're feeling bad about themselves and then they all want to jump on someone else.

Others step back and don't want to engage in silly games. I really hope that's you!

Basically, anyone who creates a presence online has to accept the fact that the cyberbullies are going to do the stupid things they're going to do. Hopefully we can change their minds someday, but before we fix them, we have to make sure we fix ourselves and learn that we can handle a few dumb haters.

HOW TO DEAL WITH CYBERBULLIES

1 Don't take it personally, as I already said.

I roll my eyes at how lame these bullies are. They aren't funny or original or smart. Most of them can hardly put a verb and a noun in the same sentence. They're not the kind of people I'd ever want to have in my life, so who cares what they think? They're losers.

If you do think someone you know is doing the bullying, ask the person first, to their face, before you do anything.

I bet you know already how easy it is to change someone's name in a phone to someone else's in order to fake a conversation. Or how easy it is to Photoshop a quick mean tweet. I mean, I could have a conversation with Harry Styles right now if I changed my mom's name in my phone to Harry Styles!

So this makes me leery about text messages. It's really hard to know what's real and what's not, because you can change them (and your identity) so easily and lie about things on social media. If you want to make someone look bad, you can even delete your own mean messages to them and make them seem like the villains when they were only responding to the awful things you might have said. It's messed up!

If you think that the messages you're getting aren't real, or that you've been hacked, don't text the people in the threads. Pick up the phone and make an actual call to sort it out.

3 **Adults can step in at any time to help you.**

If you are getting seriously bullied—and I really, really hope you aren't!—do not suffer in silence. Any cyberbullying that takes place during school hours can and should be dealt with by the school. (Although, I have to say, I am still deeply disappointed with my high school for not taking the Senior Seconds list more seriously and actually trying harder to find out the idiot culprits behind it. They really dropped the ball.) If not, discuss your options for taking action with your parents or adults you trust. Bullies need to understand that actions have consequences!

Unfortunately, sometimes adults don't know how to handle problems that we go through, especially online bullying, so the courage and motivation to block out the haters ultimately has to come from inside you. Please don't let it get to you. You are amazing, and these haters are just looking for someone to take out their own problems on.

As Teala and I love to say, just say, "No promo!" It basically means we don't care to give haters any attention, because that's all they want—so when someone decides to come hating at us, we just laugh and say, "Sorry, you can try all you want, but no promo!"

CHAPTER 10

My BIGGEST CHALLENGE, and HOW I PUSHED THROUGH IT

fter my breakup with JC in junior year, I was feeling kind of rebellious. I was fresh off my relationship ending, and during the time with JC, he had opened my world up to a whole different crowd of people who partied, and they all drove cars. It was weird, because I still had my little group of best friends who ate lunch with me and played video games after school with me, yet I was getting invited to all the parties and hangouts with JC's group. I felt kind of

sexier, since JC was the first boy that I had consistently and scandalously made out with, and when it ended, I kept that feeling of being "on top of the world" with me. I think I was looking for something to make me feel good again, since JC and I had ended. That's where the story starts.

In came a classmate I'll call Brian. Brian was another one of those boys who a lot of kids in school talked about. He was gorgeous. It wasn't just his eyes, his hair, his complexion, his smile. It was all of them. And of course he was a star athlete.

I had become friends with Brian back in freshman year, when he sat in front of me in one of my classes. I, like virtually every other girl in the nearest ten-mile radius, thought Brian was hot, and melted over his wide and pearly white smile. We became good friends, because as you know from earlier, I was way too interested in Ben to go chasing after anyone else—especially Brian. Besides, Brian was too cool for me, anyway!

I think Brian liked that I didn't really "want" him, because he became sort of my good friend. He'd always talk to me and seemed like he really cared to know about things going on in my life, like my eventual relationship with Ben. We got along well, which in turn made a lot of jealous girls not like me. I even once got a threatening Facebook message (yes, a girl FACEBOOK MESSAGED ME) telling me to stay away from Brian because this girl "liked him." I was like . . . . okay . . . ?

Things were going really well for Brian up until sophomore year, when one day everything changed. BRIAN HAD GOTTEN EXPELLED! It turned out that Brian smoked weed, and I didn't even know this because I was totally oblivious to drugs and parties until . . . well, basically still now . . . He tried to sell weed on campus and had gotten caught, and in turn he was sent to a continuation home school.

A whole year went by without Brian. It was almost as if people forgot about him, but then suddenly junior year was midway through and Brian was allowed back onto campus. Even though he remained sort of low-key, a lot of the same girls still wanted him. Even I did too a little, but now I was single, which was something that I definitely wasn't back in freshman year, and Brian knew that.

Now, back to how I was feeling after JC cheated on me. I was feeling HOT. I was feeling popular. I was feeling like I needed to redeem my title (whatever that was) after being cheated on, and suddenly I got a text on my crappy little pay-as-you-go phone . . . and it was Brian!

Brian: *Hey, what are you doing? Let's hang out. I want to see you.*

Wow. Brian. The bad boy that tons of girls wanted, and he was texting me to hang out.

It was Monday, a school night, and I had a math test the next day. My math teacher was one of those "cool" teachers, and so the night before every test, she would meet our class at the local Panera Bread to eat and have a study session over pasta and lemonade. I knew I shouldn't be making plans with anyone to hang out, but it was hot Brian, and this opportunity didn't happen often or to just anyone.

So I tried to compromise.

Eva: *I can't hang out tonight, I have a test tomorrow for Mrs. Jackson! What about tomorrow?*

Brian: *I can't tomorrow. Only tonight. Can I pick you up after your study session?*

Eva: *I can't, I have to study! What if you just come to my study session? Mrs. Jackson is super cool and won't mind you being there. It's literally just Panera, we're all just eating and studying.*

I tried to find any way to hang out with him while fitting in my study session. I thought it could be really cool if I showed up to the study session with hot Brian by my side just watching me study. I could study AND hang out with someone so hot. It was perfect. I was really, really hoping he'd agree to his idea.

Brian: *I can't. What if I just pick you up before your study session and we could get pizza nearby?*

Brian was a slick kind of guy. He knew all the right things to say to convince a girl to fall right into his hands. He was the type of guy to convince a girl to go outside in negative 20-degree weather while wearing a swimsuit, talking about how "it's not that bad." When he said he wanted to hang out beforehand, I figured it was a compromise I could manage, and so I let him win this one. He was to pick me up at Panera at around 4 p.m., and we'd hang out until my study session an hour later! Brian sent me some flirty mes-

sage after I agreed, and I got butterflies in my stomach. It was pretty obvious he was into me, and I was excited to maybe have the chance to kiss him. I'd never kissed someone that hot. Not even JC had been that hot!

Brian picked me up in his parents' SUV, and I got into the passenger seat. I felt so mature. He seemed so interested in me. He made me feel so cool. I smiled and buckled my seat belt, preparing to head off to a nearby pizza parlor. We started driving and I—since I considered myself pretty close to Brian (having been a friend to him since freshman year)—asked him about the whole "expelled situation" for the first time.

Brian started telling me all about how he'd had a "religious journey while being expelled." He told me how he realized how dumb he had been "back in sophomore year" and how "drugs are such a dumb thing to do and are so in the past." I was so proud of him. Like, wow, Brian had actually learned something from his mistakes! I was beaming. Here I was, sitting in the passenger seat of his parents' car, smiling. Maybe Brian wasn't so bad after all?

It was then that I looked out the window and noticed that I didn't recognize where we were. At all. I mean, we were in my hometown—which I thought I knew every in and out of—but I definitely had agreed only to getting pizza nearby . . . and there was no pizza parlor in sight. Instead, we were heading in the direction of what seemed to be a collection of various warehouses and empty business buildings.

"What's going on?" I said "I thought we were getting pizza?"

Brian didn't say anything back. He didn't even look at me.

All of a sudden we were parking, but not in a parking spot. I looked around and noticed we were in a little pocket of the back of a business building, right next to a thick wall covered in bushes and a dumpster. I look at the building and noticed one word on a sign.

CHURCH

We had parked behind a church?

It was awkwardly quiet. Nobody was saying a word, and then all of a sudden Brian looked me in the eye and leaned in for a kiss. I leaned in closer and kissed him back, and we started making out. He took my shirt off and started aggressively touching me, and I was suddenly scared. Something didn't feel right. This was way too much for me.

"Have sex with me," Brian said.

WHAT?!?!?!

"NO!" I blurted out, at first laughing at his proposal. "Why would I have sex with you?"

"Because you want to!" he replied.

"No, I don't. What would make you think I would, ever?"

"Come on, Eva, you totally want it. I could tell by the way you texted me!"

"That I wanted to eat pizza before my study session? Seriously, Brian. Okay, the joke is over."

"But, Eva, come onnnn, please?"

"No!"

At this point, I was thinking that if I just kept making it very clear that there was no way in hell's kitchen I was about to have sex with this boy, he would get all embarrassed and definitely stop asking.

"Why not?" he pleaded.

"I'm a VIRGIN!!!"

"No you're not . . . I know you're not."

Okay, what?

"I. Am. A. VIIIIIIRGIN," I proclaimed with dignity. Hello? I'd been through a LOT. I was CHEATED on because I wanted to stay a virgin, and now all of a sudden this boy was trying to tell me otherwise? OH HELL NO.

"I know you had sex with Ben."

Okay, wait, WHAT THE HELL. First of all, Ben was the LAST person I would have expected him to say I had lost my virginity to. I mean, Ben and I barely kissed with the lights off. Ben and I ate our lunch out of paper sacks on the grass. Ben and I watched Disney movies for fun on Friday nights. Where was this coming from???

"No, I didn't!" I said. I was livid.

At this point, we had been sitting there for way too long, and he was going back and forth with me saying no and him saying yes. I was trying to figure out a way out of this. I couldn't get my shirt quickly. He had thrown it somewhere to the back of the car. I couldn't leave the car. He could have just driven off and left me in an abandoned area with no top and no phone to call for help. Or worse, if I really said no, he could even hurt me.

Twenty more minutes passed of me saying no, and he just wouldn't let up. I had run out of things to say. I was just repeating myself. He was beating me down to nothing.

"Have sex with me, okay?" he said. I started to tear up and looked down. I couldn't even say no anymore. I just said nothing.

The silence, I guess, meant okay in his eyes, and he took my pants off while I cried and didn't say a word. I didn't even help him. I just laid lifeless, covered in tearstains, in the seat while he climbed over and maneuvered through it all. He had sex with me for not even twenty seconds. It was terrible. I cried the whole time as silently as I could. He could sense I clearly was not into it and said, "Do you want me to stop?"

I still remember through my tears I choked out a muffled yes. I couldn't even look at him. He pulled the condom off and threw it into the bushes outside. He found my shirt in the back of the car and handed it to me. Then he drove me back to the study session. The whole way there he talked about how much weed he had smoked the other day. He hadn't changed one bit. I never looked at him once. He dropped me off, and I forced a smile as he said, "See ya later!" and sped off.

The moment he was gone, I burst into completely hysterical tears. I was shaking. I could barely even breathe. I was having a full-on panic attack. In my head, while I was crying, all I could hear were my jumbled thoughts going, *Did I just get raped?* So I went into the alley next to the study session and called Jenny. She was in dance class and didn't answer, so I called the only other person that really knew me: Ben. Luckily, Ben answered his phone.

I told him everything, and he told me things would be okay and to go study for my test. So I tried to study with the rest of the class, but the whole time I was numb, with tears in my eyes and everyone looking at me like I was insane. I cleaned myself up and then went home.

I went to school the next day a complete wreck. I ended up failing my math test. I walked the halls the rest of the week numb and shaking. I didn't talk to anyone at all. My life seemed like it would go on like this forever, until Thursday.

On Thursday, I was sitting in my history class when my teacher started talking and asked everyone to turn in their "letter to a soldier" care package. Basically, we were supposed to write a letter to a soldier in Iraq and send a gift to them. I had completely forgotten about it. I mean, I had forgotten to do all my homework that week. I had bombed my math test. I couldn't focus. It was all I could do to even get up and get dressed and go to school. All that was on my mind was that painful scene in the car, replaying itself over and over again.

I raised my hand and asked if I could turn it in the next day, because I had "something really bad happen earlier in the week and it's been affecting me in a hard way." My teacher, who I'd thought was generally understanding and kind of cool, turned cold on me. She looked me dead in the eye and said, "Everyone has stuff they're stressed about, Eva. You don't think I do?? But we have to keep on track and not forget assignments!" She was so rude. Keep in mind at this point the whole class is silent in their seats watching this all go down. I started to cry in the middle of class at my seat. Jenny, who was still my best friend at this point, luckily knew the whole story and spoke up for me. She said, "You don't understand, Mrs. Smith. Eva is going through a lot."

Mrs. Smith didn't seem to care. I sat in silence, crying into my backpack, feeling as if the whole world was crashing down on me. I stayed in my own little bubble until I heard Mrs. Smith say, in a not-much-kinder tone of voice, "Do you want to go to the office?" I told her that I did, and I got up, left my books and everything behind, and walked out of class until my walk turned into a run, and suddenly I was running and crying in the empty hallway with nowhere to go. Thank goodness I ran right into my favorite teacher, Mrs. Elliott, who taught literature.

Mrs. Elliott had an empty period and was alone, so luckily I had her all to myself. I told her everything. I told her that Ben and Jenny knew, so she got to Ben and asked him to come into the empty room with me, and they both held me while I told them the entire story. I felt so much better afterward. I had gotten the advice I needed, I let all the bad feelings out, and finally, *finally* felt like it was over and I could go on with my life. I left the classroom with a sliver of hope. I spent the rest of the period walking around the empty hallways of the school, while everyone else was in their classes, and that's when I heard, "Eva Gutowski, please come to the office."

I shrugged. I knew I had totally walked out of history class, so I assumed I'd be getting in trouble for that, and headed to the office to make up an excuse for why I'd ditched. When I got to the office, though, it looked less like my familiar high school office and more like a police station. Police. Were. Everywhere. (I had no idea that my teacher was a mandated reporter and had to tell the school administrators about any incidents that happened involving her students.)

I freaked out and tried to escape, until an officer looked right at me and then at a photo of me he had printed out and that he had clenched in his hand, and said, "You must be Eva. We just called your parents and they're on their way."

Oh no.

Suddenly my whole life went into blur mode. I remember being taken into a small room and sobbing to the unfriendly policeman while he asked me for Brian's height, hair color, and weight, and what car he drove. I had to tell him the whole story again, and then he told me I'd need to tell my parents AGAIN once they arrived. I remember saying, "No, you have to tell them, I'm not telling that story again, I can't, especially to my parents' faces." But then my parents showed up and we were brought back into the windowless conference room as they heard what had happened to me and they cried.

After hours at the school office, I was driven straight to the hospital, where I was ushered into the most cold, uninviting room ever and stripped naked in front of a woman who photographed me like I was an animal in a testing facility. I had to turn to

my sides with my arms up as she took flash photos of my naked body to find evidence of any bruising. They told me I had to complete a "rape kit," and this meant she had to insert a cold metal speculum inside my vagina as she took swabs for STDs. I had to take a pregnancy test to make sure he didn't get me pregnant. They took all of my clothes for the police and gave me a hospital outfit to wear home instead. I was made to feel like a quarantined animal.

After that, I immediately had to go to a therapy room with my parents as I was forced to sit down and schedule rape counseling. I begged my parents not to do it. I said I didn't need it and they protested, until finally I just declared I wouldn't go to it if they tried.

As soon as that was over, I was driven to the police station, where I was given an officer assigned to my "case." Great, so now I had a case.

The next three months were spent in and out of the police station. All I wanted to do was move on, but the police were now involved, and every two weeks I had to go there to talk about my rape once again and help the case. I had to go home and gather my jeans, sweater, and even my underwear because it was "evidence," and I had to give it all to the police. I never got them back.

Meanwhile, I was still in school with Brian.

Finally, one night, my police officer had me call Brian's phone, which was tapped into from the station, and I got him to admit, on the phone, what he had done. He was so relaxed about it. He didn't even care. He thought I was stupid for even calling him about it, since it had happened months ago. He said, "Yeah, I guess I took advantage of you." Like it had been nothing. I cried. He had SAID it. I was going to be okay! The police officer said I wouldn't need to worry anymore, and that they would come to my school within the next three days to get him out.

I went back to school. I was nervous for the first day, then the third day, but then more and more days went by and Brian was still most definitely in my classes. The police never came. Never did *anything*. We went back to the station to ask what had happened, and no one talked to us. It was said that there was a child abuse case that was "more important and a stronger case" that my assigned officer was busy with. And so that was it. I never heard anything more, and the police became unresponsive. The school didn't do a single thing. They never even called me back into the office.

I was left to get through this on my own, and so I did.

This was an important lesson for me in the art of forgiveness.

When people do horrible, terrible things to you, your first way to cope is to hate them. But hate is a terrible feeling. It almost ends up hurting you just as much as you think it'll hurt them. Hating someone for what they did wrong isn't a permanent way to get over something and rise above it.

Instead, you have to forgive.

It sucks, yes, that we have to work hard to find in ourselves a way to forgive someone for what they brought upon us. Especially if we were wholly innocent in whatever situation.

The only way I got through this and became able to talk about it without bursting into tears was being able to process that:

 People can do horrible things.

People make mistakes, and some people can't seem to stop making the same mistakes over and over again. And somewhere along their line of messing up, you fall in, and you become the victim of those mistakes. But mistakes, no matter how small or how big, are just mistakes. And you have to forgive people for making them not just for them, but more importantly for yourself.

 Everyone does what they do for a reason, and everyone's actions have a reason behind them.

Whether it's something completely terrible that happened in their lives when they were ten, or whether they're going through something hard in that moment, or whether they're just selfish people who care only about themselves, those things affect them and shape who they become. "Bad" people aren't just born "bad." They go through things. They constantly get knocked down. They go through so much hurt that suddenly "hurt" becomes a normal thing to feel and reflect.

Hurt can change you and mold you into a really dark, evil person, and do that really quickly. If you're super strong, you can avoid turning into a messed-up person, but deep down, you never forget a terrible memory, and in some way small or large, you take that with you for the rest of your life.

I'm strong. I have seen hurt. I've felt hurt. I've seen terrible things, and yet I still manage to smile and look on the bright side, but for a lot of people it isn't that easy. And I can't blame someone for hurting me because of them not being strong enough to help themselves.

3 It is NOT your fault!

This is the most important thing, because it's something everyone decides to think when they go through something traumatic. "It was my fault," they say. "If only I had . . ."

No, it was not.

To process what happened to me, I started to blame myself. I would say to myself, "Well, Eva you're so dumb, you should have never gotten in the car," and, "Eva, you are so stupid, you should have known he wasn't changed into a new person," and, "Eva, you should have never even kissed him. You asked for it by teasing him," and, "Eva, you should never have let him take off your shirt." This only made things worse.

I think I started to blame myself because I was embarrassed about looking helpless. I didn't like everyone feeling sorry for me. I felt like they didn't believe the real story, anyway, so I had to just accept what everyone else was thinking and blame myself so that it could be over with. It wasn't until I realized, *Hey, Eva, STOP!* EVERYONE blames themselves! It's one of the five stages of getting over things!

If you are ever going through a traumatic experience, know that when you start to blame yourself, it's just a stage. It sounds funny and cliché, but it really is true. I blamed myself for just about every little thing until I realized that you can find reasons to blame yourself for just about anything that goes wrong in your life. I can find ways to blame my best friend failing her math test on myself. "I shouldn't have hung out with her on Friday—then she could have studied more." Or "I should have asked her to come over while

I was studying. I shouldn't have texted her so much the night before the test."

In reality, this is ridiculous. You look out for yourself. You take care of your actions and who you are shaped to be. Someone else's bad intentions are their bad intentions, and they will find ways to take them out regardless of all the good decisions you make. You just have to remember to look out for yourself as best as you can, and be ready to continue to look out for yourself whenever occasional bad things may strike.

Stay strong, and know that you can and will get through anything.

I forgave Brian months after it happened. I had moved on as best as I could, and finished up my junior year. I had to endure my entire rest of high school with him, and I graduated right alongside him. I thought about telling the whole school what he did to me. I thought about writing BRIAN RAPED ME in black Sharpie in the bathroom stall. One day, I went to pee in the sports locker bathroom once and saw BRIAN IS THE BEST SEX EVER on the stall's wall, and almost passed out/threw up (not joking).

Before all this had happened, I had seen my parents do wrong. They argued and sometimes even got physical while I watched with my own eyes, which hurt me a lot. I thought that was God challenging me. I thought that was the pivotal thing I'd have to go through in my life.

But Brian was different. Brian was my own pain I had to deal with. Brian was MY moment to learn how to heal.

So I moved on. I graduated strong, proud, accepted to college. I graduated with purpose and a smile on my face. I knew I could have *not* graduated. I could have let my rape consume me and kill my dreams and my goals. I mean, I really did feel worthless afterward, and those feelings and that trauma lingered for months. But I prevailed, and I made a damn good life for myself.

I wanted to share this story so badly, because as I got older, I started to see more girls with the exact same story as mine. I started to see way too many girls on the news and in magazines being brave enough to share their story and then watched them be knocked down by the media and even by their own schools, trying to paint them as liars. I started to see more cases of the police dismissing these rapes as not important enough to follow up on. Girls were getting raped and abused by quarterbacks of star football team schools or swim team stars, and there was no one to believe them or help them. And I knew that feeling. I know exactly how it feels to be wronged by the person everybody thinks is perfect. And it is *hard*.

Once I started to see so many girls going through the same pain and story that I went through, I started to cry, every time. Up until this exact day, I still get so emotional about this, and it's not even because of my situation. It's about all those other girls. I always would tell myself God wouldn't have given me this burden if he knew I couldn't handle it. God knew that I would be not only strong enough to prevail and push past and come out on top of my rape, but he also knew that he would bless me with my dreams being fulfilled. He knew I would eventually have a large voice that people would listen to, and he gave me a mountain to climb in high school so that in turn I could help people who have to climb that same mountain in the future and have no one to turn to for guidance.

Too many people are too harsh on others because they simply have never been in their shoes before. Girls who are open about their rapes are not open because they want people to "feel sorry for them" or get famous for it. Girls are open because they want justice, and justice is not being served.

Girls are being treated in disgusting ways by people that have never been in their shoes before—but I have walked the same path they are walking, and I never got justice. My justice is being able to show everyone reading this book that all of the stories you keep hearing on TV or are seeing online are in fact true, and I am part of the growing list of too many girls who aren't taken seriously when they try to get help from the people who are meant to help them.

I may have not gotten justice from Brian, or from my community, but to this day, I am the victor. I have won. My life is so amazing. I have amazing friends, an amazing family who love me, and an amazing cat named Paris. My job allows me to spread important messages like this, and that's all I needed to feel good. To heal. To move on.

Brian, not surprisingly, is still involved with drugs and screwing girls over. His girlfriend and I are actually friends, and I've talked her through some tough times she's had with him. I still see his Facebook posts every week. I could have easily let this moment in my life tear me down and bring me to nothing, and I did for a little bit. But it was the drive I had to make sure my life turned out a happier story than his that pushed me to go forward and to forgive, and I am still pushing today.

My life is MyLifeAsEva. I live my life and push through tough times for my viewers to know that they can too, and now they know that if I can get through the most unjust, darkest moment of my life, they can get through it too.

EATING

HEALTHY

CHAPTER 11

HEALTH

igh school just as it is is embarrassing enough. Honestly, after all the things that happened to me just in freshman year alone, you'd think God would be like, "Okay, this girl has had enough embarrassment for the year. Y'all can take a break, embarrassment angels! See ya!"

Seriously, like the second week of freshman year I peed my pants from laughing too hard in drama class . . . and had to walk across campus trying to hide my pee stain with my backpack. I am not kidding. I literally lowered that little buckle thing on my backpack straps as low as they could go to hide my pee pants.

I thought I'd be able to get by in high school by being embarrassed about the normal stuff. You know, slipping on a wet floor when hurrying down the hall in between periods, or being called out for not bringing my textbook. Easy things.

Never in my life did I think I'd be embarrassed because of health issues.

It's kind of expected of you when you're young that you'll be healthy. We're told to eat our vegetables, take vitamins, exercise three times a week, and we'll live happily ever after. But that's not always the case. And the thing is, you shouldn't have to deal with health issues at a young age, and unless you're bleeding profusely from your kneecap after wiping out on your skateboard, you're probably not in a hurry to get to the nearest doctor's office just to say hi and maybe score a free lollipop. It's hard enough just being a kid. It's not expected for a kid to be hospitalized. I was a little different.

It all started when I was young. I remember being around seven years old, visiting Arizona with my family, and it was late at night. Somehow, I ended up passing out and being rushed to the hospital and having to get a bunch of IVs stuck in me. That was so long ago, but I still remember the feeling I had of being confused as to why this was happening to me. I didn't know what I'd done wrong.

Fast-forward seven years later, to when I was fourteen. The fainting spells had become chronic, and for years I'd dealt with unexplainable passing-out in random places, like malls or theme parks or showers, almost on a monthly basis. It consumed my life, especially because it nearly always happened in public places, around my friends or family. I would try so hard to not let myself pass out, which would lead to me awkwardly sitting on a floor, hiding my face in between my legs, mortified for people to see me fighting so hard to not keel over in a dead faint.

The feeling was and still is unexplainable. It always starts off with a hot, dizzy feeling. And then suddenly everything becomes warm and hard to see. Suddenly I'm stricken with a massive headache, and it seems as if every part of my body can whisper in a mean and frantic hissing noise, and all parts are telling me to "SIT DOWN, LIE DOWN, FIND A SEAT NOW, FAST, OR ELSE." My mind becomes Jell-O and all I can think about is, *Oh no, it's happening, I need to find a place to be alone.* I gasp for air but can't seem to find it, and this is around the time that all my friends around me will start to ask, "Eva, what's wrong? Are you okay?" but even if I weren't just about to pass out, I couldn't possibly explain to them what's going on with me.

So I would struggle find a place to sit, and normally I would just settle on the floor. I'd try to fight it and start blinking a lot, but with every blink I'd open my eyes and see less and less, and then I'd close my eyes, open them again, and only see black. And then I'd have to lie down and be still.

This was my life. And then there I was, starting my freshman year of high school.

By that time, I was determined to get to the bottom of these horrible fainting spells, so at first I tried to solve the mystery myself. My grandpa was diabetic, and he had this blood pressure machine he could use in the house, that always sat on the kitchen table. Because my grandpa had to test his blood-sugar levels every day, he let me test mine, especially when I'd start to feel dizzy, and I saw that my own levels were extremely low—way below normal.

I started to think maybe I could be diabetic, and then for a split second, I was happy, because Jesse Soto, my junior high school crush, also happened to be diabetic, and I thought maybe that would make him like me finally. But I quickly shook that idea out of my head and moved on. I didn't want to scare myself and diagnose myself with something I had absolutely no idea about.

At the time, as you know, I was really getting into dance. I danced every day, for nearly four hours a day. I'd dance in the morning for class, then I'd dance all during lunch, and then I'd dance after school. Dance classes were when I started to realize more things were a little weird about me.

Winter came, and Southern California dropped to a not-so-frigid temperature of 52 degrees. I could probably still have fried a damn egg on the concrete. I had dance class at seven in the morning, and we'd always leave the doors open to the dance room for some strange reason. I remember I couldn't even dance properly for the whole winter season, because the dance floor made my feet so cold that they would turn purple and yellow and numb. My feet would ache because of the cold floors, as if I were walking through snow for five miles, yet it was only 52 degrees outside. Way too warm

for cold sensitivity. People would make fun of my feet for turning purple. I tried fuzzy socks under dance shoes, but that didn't work at all, and I ended up looking ridiculous. Still, it was the best I could do.

Around this same time, during freshman year, my period was also absolutely terrible, to the point that the pain was so bad that I would literally cry in my bed, writhing around and waiting for the cramps to end. My period would make me THROW UP, and one time I had my period and threw up *seventeen* times . . . Yes, you read that right . . . That was the moment I went to my parents and begged for actual medical help.

My mom had pretty good health insurance because of her job at the time, so I was able to get an appointment at a really nice hospital right up the street from my house. I would finally be able to explain to a doctor what all my symptoms were. I would tell them everything that was wrong with me. I felt so hopeful. Finally, this would all be fixed.

A week later, when I sat in the doctor's office, they explained to me that they would do some blood work, and in about two weeks' time, they would know what was going on. I was a little scared at first. I mean, blood work? Hello, I knew that this was 2008, and *Twilight* was all the rage back then, but I was not into getting my blood sucked, sorry, ma'am. Still, I let them do it. I mean, I was determined to just get this over and done with and have a diagnosis and finally live a normal, stable life.

Except things didn't go as planned. Two weeks later, the blood work came in, and the doctors were stumped. They had guesses, but no idea what could be happening. A ton of ideas were being passed around, and the only way to solve it was to keep doing more blood tests. Le sigh. Okay, fine.

This cycle went on for longer than I could have ever expected. It literally became a routine. Go to the hospital, get blood work done, wait two weeks for an answer, no answer, and repeat and repeat and repeat.

No one could ever figure out what was wrong or why this was happening to me. I didn't feel sick, but I didn't feel all right, either. And that was even scarier.

The scariest part was that no one could see anything wrong, at least by looking at me. Aside from my feet, I seemed perfectly normal. I danced like an athlete. I worked hard. I had a group of friends. And yet I was going through so much on the inside, and no one could sympathize.

Freshman year ended and I went with my sister to New York City to visit our relatives for much of the summer. The week before school was about to start, we were still in New York when my pathetic little pay-as-you-go phone rang. I knew I'd be wasting valuable go-phone minutes answering the call, but luckily I answered it anyway. What I heard was a message from the hospital saying that "Oh, by the way, we're just calling to say your daughter needs to have an MRI done. As soon as possible. Okay. Thanks so much. Goodbye."

Obviously, they meant to call my parents' phone, but they called my number instead. Apparently the doctors thought I had a tumor on my pituitary gland, and they wanted to see if it would show up on an MRI, which is a high-tech procedure where they use magnetic resonance imaging to scan your brain.

Can you imagine? There I was, sitting on a park bench eating my aunt Sandy's seedless watermelon she bought for seventy-nine cents a pound, and I was putting the puzzle pieces together. MRI? Tumor? Tumors are cancer, right? You mean I might have CANCER?

I was freshly fifteen years old. I didn't know anything about this stuff. I was freaking out. Who wouldn't? I was like, Okay, Eva, now you have cancer in your brain. Oh, cool, you're going to die! And I wasn't even home where I could go see my friends and have a big cry and get some support. I had to wait till we flew home, go to my first day of sopho-more year, and then, the moment school ended, go get tested. And the whole time I was sure I was done for.

The MRI was done at a big scary hospital in Anaheim. To get an MRI, the doctors inject you with an ink that goes to your brain, and then they stick you in a human toaster machine where you have to lie completely still and listen to the gentle sounds of harsh beeping and grinding, and the internal sounds of your mind telling you this is the next step on your pathway to a certain death. The ink sloshes around in your brain, and based on where the ink seeps, the doctors can tell if there are any abnormalities. Like tumors, for example.

A week later, the results arrived and the doctors yet again said they didn't find anything. They told me maybe there still was a tumor, but it was just too small to detect yet. Or possibly this maybe-tumor was benign. Oh. *Thanks*. Was that sup-posed to make me feel better?

The economy still wasn't doing too well for working-class families like my own, and shortly after this, my mom lost her job, which meant that we lost the good health insurance. Suddenly it was back to square one. The only thing that was getting me through high school was knowing that, eventually, if I kept getting tested, someday someone would figure

out what was wrong with me. But with-out insurance, the testing would have to stop. It was extremely expensive, and we just couldn't afford it.

So I spent the rest of high school wondering if I had a brain tumor or not. Every time I fainted, I thought it was due to some hidden little tumor that was going to kill me. Maybe it was growing, but I didn't have a doctor who could check and do more blood work. Not only could no one figure out the prob-lem, but now no one was interested in figuring out the problem but me.

I still remember one night after dance class, I had another moment where I was close to passing out, so I con-vinced my parents to take me to urgent care, where the only person available to look at me was a children's pediatrician named Greta. I tried to explain to her my whole medical history. I was helpless and frantic. I needed answers. I told her all about me passing out since I was a kid, my feet being so cold and turning purple and yellow, my super-low blood sugar. She looked at me with a dead glare, blinked her eyes, and had the nerve to say, "Maybe if you wore pants in cold weather you wouldn't have poor blood circulation. Also, you should eat more to avoid passing out. You look thin." I looked down. I was wearing my required dance practice uniform: a racer-back tank and monogrammed shorts. EXCUSE ME, GRETA?!?!? I literally rushed from practice to get medical attention and all this doctor could tell me to do was to eat more and put pants on.

I looked over at my mom and gave her my most offended look, blinking back tears. But then my mom did the last thing I expected. My mom smiled and agreed. WITH GRETA?!?

I burst into tears and literally ran out of the urgent care room. I stormed off to the car where I screamed and cried at my mom, pleading with her to do something, anything. I mean, how could they possibly listen to that awful Greta, after knowing everything that I'd been through for so many years. Put pants on and eat more?! THAT WASN'T THE ISSUE AND THEY KNEW IT. I think my parents felt bad that we didn't have proper health insurance to help me, and so they tried to avoid the problem, thinking that it would somehow magically disappear.

By the time I was a senior, I wasn't fainting quite as much, but there was still no resolution to the whole tumor thing. And we still didn't have the health insurance for me to be able to fix myself. I had to find ways to deal with my condition, so I started figuring out my own little DIY ways to avoid passing out. These tricks also made me feel like I was more in control of my health problems. I would

buy diabetic socks to keep my feet warm in dance, and the socks would hide my numb, cold, purple feet. I would make sure I was always hydrated and well fed. I would do whatever I could to combat every single thing that could possibly be wrong with me. And this worked pretty well, but all the way up until college and even now, I still occasionally go through the same familiar and scary moments of knowing I'm about to pass out, that awful feeling that I wish I hadn't grown up with.

I have good medical insurance now, and even though I hate the doctor's office, I have learned how important it is to care about the little things that tip you off. These things matter tremendously, and just because you can't "see" a problem in yourself doesn't mean that you're crazy when you feel like something is off. It's the hardest thing to have something different about you that no one else can see, because it makes it hard for people to understand what you're going through, and oftentimes people just don't care and are quick to judge you.

For example, a close friend of mine struggled in school for years and years until finally, when it was almost too late, she realized she had dyslexia. And the whole time, she knew something must have been wrong, but she was too scared to admit that she thought she might need help. I grew up with friends who were always picked on for having "weird personalities," and it wasn't until after they graduated that they realized they had personality disorders or even were bipolar. It sucks that sometimes we have to go through the struggle of trying to figure out things about ourselves, and that the struggle is prolonged for so long simply because we were too scared or confused to talk about it!

You have a right to care about yourself and your health, and you don't need to feel embarrassed about going up to someone and saying, "Hey, something isn't right with me. I need your help to figure out what's going on."

As you get older, you will realize how many people have issues going on beyond what the eye can see, which is exactly why you really shouldn't judge a person for something they're doing. There's a reason behind every action. Let your reason behind your action of shaking off the haters and helping the ones who need help be simply that you care about them and want them to have the same happiness that you found.

Every day I still go through being scared that my fainting episodes will come back, but I'm now open about it. In school, I didn't know how to explain to people what was going on, and so they'd judge me because they didn't understand and make quick excuses for why I

was acting a certain way. I still don't know how to explain to people what's going on—and I still haven't gotten a firm and comprehensive diagnosis of what has caused my health issues—but now I have such a better mind-set regarding such things because I know that's just me, and it doesn't change who I am. I keep looking for a doctor or medical professional who will put all the pieces together. But I'm okay. Most of all, it doesn't own me.

If you're going through anything where you feel scared to speak up because you don't think anyone will understand, know that there are people who *do* understand and will help you. You just have to take the first leap into being confident enough to say what's scaring or worrying you, and let the others do their best for you!

DEPRESSION

Freshman year, despite all the fun things I did with my friends, and all the memories I made with Ben, and the eventful moments at school, I still felt a little sad overall.

While everything was basically going okay at school, at home I was a mess. And I think that always carried over into my life, because how could I be 100 percent there for everything when I had so much on my mind going on about what was going on behind closed doors?

How could I make friends, be there for them, be a best friend, and get good grades when it felt like a huge piece of me was missing? I often walked around feeling like I had a giant hole in my chest.

I was dealing with a lot of pain because my family was having problems at home. There were bad financial problems. There was also a lot of arguing going on, and a lot of stress was put on me because of it. Combine all the arguing with no space to be alone, because we were a family of four sharing a one-bedroom apartment. For some months, my bedroom was the living room couch with my sister. We'd put together change to get a cup of noodles from the liquor store for dinner, and getting lucky meant having enough money to buy a microwave burrito.

I could never invite friends over, which affected me a lot, since we grew up in a pretty wealthy neighborhood. I became hyperaware of class differences, especially because of the bread van.

Let me explain: When he was still a student, my grandpa had wanted to be a history professor, but he ditched it to work for nonprofits. For the last forty-five years, my grandfather and my grandmother have worked for an organization where they feed homeless people. Grandpa's job is feeding them every meal, and making sure they have clothes on their backs, and getting kids out of gangs. It has always been very rewarding work, but it is not a well-paying career (although it should be!).

What comes with that low salary is no money to afford a proper vehicle. Instead, they drive the large volunteer vans—which seat fourteen to seventeen people—that this organization uses to bring low-income children to camps in Big Bear, and to ferry others around as needed.

Every few days my grandpa would have to go to our local grocery stores to "get the bread." The bread and the baked goods that were day-old (and still good) or about to expire were donated to food banks and shelters instead of being thrown out. This is truly a good cause, and I really loved my grandpa for having such a worthy job, but I have to admit the vans always smelled like bread. Don't get me wrong—I love bread. But after years of the bread runs, the vans took on a very particular, yeasty stink! And there would always be that single donut or muffin rolling around on the floor or seat that got loose, so I'd inevitably either sit on it or step in it. Not a good look!

The vans were so ugly (they were either white or this sort of ugly dull metallic baby blue) and smelled so bad that being driven around in them over the years was pretty disgusting and uncomfortable. They got really dirty and dusty from the bread and even the outsides were filthy. One day some stupid kid drew a swastika on the dusty back window of one of the vans, and I had to get a ladder to wipe it off. So it was always a super-lucky day when Grandma was driving the van and Grandpa could drive me to school in an old truck that was nearly as disgusting, but not quite.

This was in Orange County, remember, which is one of the richest areas in this country. My classmates were getting dropped off in Range Rovers and convertibles and nice minivans with doors that automatically opened. Not in stinky vans that had brakes so bad you could hear the *EEEEEE* screech a block away.

As a result, I was always hanging at other people's houses, but the second a friend wanted to just run up and use my bathroom, I'd panic, because our apartment, and especially the bathroom, was such an embarrassment.

I could never keep up with how perfect everyone else appeared to be, yet it seemed like everyone in my town expected *me* to be perfect, just like them, and that was extremely hard.

What I'm getting to is that I just felt a little out of place, as I think most teenagers do at some point in high school. (And not just in school, but at many times in their lives.) Once I went to college and got my own apartment, the situation that was causing a lot of my depression ended.

Consider yourself really lucky to be thrown into high school and make it out without having any bouts of sadness or self-doubt or worries. For most people, it doesn't come that easy, so if you feel like you're not really surviving in high school, please please *please* don't worry. That's NORMAL. We all figure it out as time goes on. I was just trying to survive, and I figured it out.

Here are some tips I relied on to deal with my depression:

1 I made lists!

Every time I felt like I wasn't any closer to where I wanted to be in life, I wrote down all my goals and aspirations both big and small. Then I started with small things on the list that I could accomplish within my means, like making a bouquet of flowers and putting them in my bike basket, or sewing together a sweater.

2 Speaking of sewing, KEEP YOURSELF OCCUPIED!

Do whatever you can to escape what's causing you pain. This means if you have friends down the street, go ride your bike to their house. If you have a soccer ball, take a walk to the park and kick it around. Whenever I felt empty inside, I could never even drag myself to get out of bed. I would stay in bed until sometimes even 3 p.m. before getting up. The only thing that got me out of bed was motivating myself to go do things I enjoyed. I would often take my dog for walks or even skateboard to the donut shop down the street, and if I was lucky, on some days my grandma would let me take her old shirts and cut and sew them up into new clothes. I would always go, "Grandma, you got the scraps?" and she'd know exactly what I meant and return from her room with a trash bag full of old clothes and a sewing kit.

3. Remember that perfect moments are not handed to you—they are created.

You can't wait for the perfect moment in your life where every aspect comes together to be happy. You can't sit around saying, "No, I'm not going to try today because this, this, and that went wrong, and now it's not how I want it to be." No matter what the circumstances, your day constantly has reset buttons as you go about it. Don't let a little setback define the rest of your day, week, or even year! Hit the reset button. Reset your outlook on the day and move forward with a fresh mind-set.

Here's another one of my weird Eva analogies. Think about the ocean. Think about sharks. I mean, sharks are the lions of the ocean! They're strong, they're fearsome, they have life pretty easy, and most important—they're at the top of the food chain (except for humans), and that makes them safe from predators.

Well, we can't all be sharks, and we can't all be at the top of the food chain—and that's okay. Think about how many fish there are in the sea. Think about how many fish aren't sharks! Fish that have to work harder and swim faster . . . and guess what, they survive! In a sea full of sharks, somehow the ocean still thrives, and every creature in it makes it on their own. Honestly, sharks bully dolphins, and dolphins band together and kick sharks' asses sometimes, so if anything, you should want to be a dolphin in high school. Do your own thing, have fun, get your stuff sorted, and when a shark comes around looking for trouble, show them how strong you are. But then go back to being just a happy lil' dolphin . . .

Okay, back to the story . . .

SENIOR

Paris

YEAR

CHAPTER 12

Glo–Up Level, SENIOR STYLE

kay, so you're probably thinking, Senior year, FINALLY, Eva must have figured it out! WRONG. Senior year rolled around and my glo-up still was less than amazing. I still was rocking my vampire teeth, but I think the most important thing to note was by this time, I'd started to love every little thing about myself, and felt comfortable rocking who I was. I didn't think so much about what I could fix about myself. I started just dressing in clothes I liked and doing my hair how I wanted to. The difference between junior and senior years was finding my own style. Like a lot of dresses with tights underneath instead of me trying to be a mini version of a newscaster.

I was accepting myself. I still shopped at thrift stores, I still painted my nails with polka dots, and I still wore basically no makeup, but I loved the way I looked and it wasn't even something I paid attention to, really. Sometimes I even found sundresses in my favorite thrift shops and wore them to school and looked like the conservative suburban white person that I most definitely was not! But I liked them and that's all that mattered.

So when homecoming court came around and I didn't have the money to buy five dresses, no prob. I bought two new, found two at the Goodwill, and borrowed one from an old friend.

Senior year also came with a lot of dress-up days, so I had to put my DIY skills to work. Even though I wasn't some

Betty Crocker seamstress, I held my own. From Toga Day to Senior Dress-Up Day, I still slayed. Here are some of my best fool-proof and easy Senior Dress-Up Day DIYs:

Toga Day—*basically all you need is an old satin sheet that's big enough to wrap around your body.*

Senior Old People Day—*rock out with a curly wig, a cane, and glasses, and you're good to go. This is all about the acting, not the outfit!*

Halloween—*do as you like!*

I went back to my mistake of wearing attachable ponytails and hairpieces, and even though we thought I had graduated from the poop pony, I actually just found a new alternative—two wigs that I liked to refer to as Noodle and Spaghetti. They worked well, but I was a little too dependent on them to make me look good. My moves weren't as full-out as they should have been during dance because I was worried that Noodle and Spaghetti would fly off my head.

Every day I had to tuck my hair in weird ways to make Noodle and Spaghetti fit on my head seamlessly. The problem was I had so much thick, curly hair that I ended up looking less like Gretchen Wieners and more like Jimmy Neutron.

Luckily, Noodle and Spaghetti only lasted until around Halloween time, because I quickly realized how crazy my head probably looked. I moved on to some modest dark clip-in extensions, which I sewed myself to save money.

Bye-bye, poop pony!

cute

CHAPTER 13

COLLEGE

ll my life I grew up literally worshipping football. It was what my grandpa watched every morning, and all day on Sundays. It was a way of life. My dad played football, my cousins played football, but since my parents had two girls and no boys, the closest thing they could get to the dream of their son getting a football scholarship was to have their daughter get an academic scholarship to the most coveted Orange County dream school, USC.

My family always wanted me to go to USC and become a lawyer. They would endlessly tell me stories of people they knew whose kids went to USC, became hotshot lawyers, and retired by thirty. But I would always tell them I didn't want to retire, because I wanted to have a job where I loved what I did. I knew I didn't love law and never would. They thought I was crazy.

My grandpa often got free USC football game tickets and would bring me with him when he could. I loved it. I felt cool. I had tons of USC apparel, scarves, and banners. There were some boys in my school who loved USC football too, so they bonded with me over my love of the game. I cheered for USC weekly and told myself that was where I'd end up for college.

But then high school started and it was really freaking hard. I'd think, This year is a new year and everyone starts off with fresh straight A's!! All I have to do is maintain them! That'll be easy! But then you miss one assignment and your grade drops to a D. Can we just talk about how this logic works??? Miss one assignment, grade drops to an F. Get A's on twenty assignments, grade goes up like 4 percent. When this happened to me, my positive mind-set would fly out the window and I'd end up sinking lower and lower in every class and frantically trying to maintain B's and C's. Like a B was considered me excelling in a class.

At the same time, I was smart enough to be in AP English and science, and I did love reading and writing, but they were very difficult subjects, and even though I was doing my best, I was slowly failing. Everyone makes you think that if you get a C you will never get into college and your life will be over. Part of the problem was that the other kids in these AP classes were all planning to go to big schools like Stanford and Harvard, and they effortlessly seemed to get A's. In AP English, we spent weeks dedicated to writing our college application essays, and I knew that the colleges I'd be applying to didn't require an essay . . . but there I sat, trying to write about my life, and my classmates were asking me to proof their essays when I knew I'd be saying, "Um, okay, you don't have to look over mine!"

At this point, I never thought I was going to get into college.

Still, my parents nagged all the time. When they asked if I was considering going to USC, I would entertain them with the thought but really knew I would never get in. When the time came to take the SAT and ACT exams, I did all the prep as best I could and I scored decently on both, but with my grades and no money, my expectations plummeted along with my confidence. I thought I'd have to go to a community college, and consoled myself with thinking that I'd go to the one in Santa Barbara that was really cool, and that would get me out of the house, but my dad wouldn't let me and told me that if I went to community college I wasn't going to be allowed to leave the neighborhood, so I planned to go to the one down the street from my house.

A few weeks later, I was in the bread van with Grandpa and my dad, and we drove by Cal State Fullerton. Grandpa pointed at it and said, "That's where Eva will go someday." Not USC. I nodded and stayed quiet while everyone else in the car chattered about college. I got so disappointed and thought I was probably not going to get in there—or anywhere.

So when the time came for me to fill out college applications, I didn't even want to bother, because I thought I would get rejected everywhere. I thought about out-of-state schools, but we couldn't afford them. My parents wouldn't even let me apply to their alma mater, Arizona State University, because they said it was too much of a party school! After a lot of fighting with them about where to go, I applied to four California state universities, including a new one in a cornfield, in Merced, where there is nothing to do. Of course my dad really wanted me to go there and focus on my academics!

Months later, when the letters started coming, I got several rejections. That was it. I was a failure. It was expected that I would get rejected by all of the schools I'd applied to, so I didn't think much of it until, all of a sudden, I got an acceptance letter to Cal State Fullerton and I was freaking out. Not only was it only a fifteen-minute drive from my house, but it was the school my parents wanted me to go to after USC. My grandpa had been right!

I was ecstatic. I felt so smart and wise, and my family was so happy for me, and my family ran out and bought Cal State Fullerton sweaters and hats. My grandpa was so happy. I could see the word *proud* written in his eyes. And when I put the new stuff on I thought, WOW, I am actually going to college! I was so proud of myself when I got to wear them on Senior College Day at school.

The moral of this story is that even when you think nothing is going to happen for you—you can't give up. I held onto that little sliver of hope pushing me to apply to college.

It would have been too easy for me to lose my confidence. I could have easily not studied for the SAT, or even not taken it at all. I could have let myself get C's and D's and graduated with a 2.0 GPA, but again it was that little sliver of hope telling me I couldn't just settle for okay. I had to at least try for what I wanted before I could fail while I still had some time to possibly succeed.

High school might feel like forever, but it's really not. You don't need straight A's to get into college. In fact, you don't need them to survive in life, at all.

COLLEGE LIFE

From raging Halloween parties, to falling in "real" love, to literally telling a guy to "STOP TRYING TO ROOFIE ME," college life had its moments, and I've learned a lot from those years. Hopefully this will help you through when it's your turn to finally face the big world outside of high school!

Going to college felt exactly how you might expect it to feel. There I was, suddenly thrown into a new campus, a new set of classes, a new set of friends, and, most of all, a new lifestyle. But this time, it didn't feel as scary as high school had. Instead, it felt exhilarating. Even though I once again failed at my first-day-of-school outfit, wearing my hair in an untidy, too-high-to-be-low, too-low-to-be-high pony. I wore light-wash flare jeans (keep in mind this was definitely 2012 and flare jeans were still very uncool), an embroidered peasant top, and dirty white Converse sneakers.

Still, at the time, I felt that my outfit was mature and adult. Honestly, my freshman-year-of-high-school first-day look was better than this. I obviously have learned nothing. Anyways . . .

I still remember the first day of college vividly. Especially seeing the naked boy.

So my best friend at the time, Stacy, was living in a dorm, and, like out of a movie, you needed to pay a visit there. It was 7 a.m., and Stacy had to get some books from her room. She said it would only take a minute, so I waited outside her door in the hallway.

Just so you know, the dorms at my school were coed buildings that went by different names, and it was almost like squads formed according to what building you were in and what floor your room was on. So you would identify people like "Oh, he's from Fig 4" or "Holly 10." On Elm 2 dwelled Stacy, and her next-door neighbors were two boys, Sam and Chad. Each floor had two communal bathrooms in the middle, and when you needed to pee or shower or for whatever reason throw up, you'd have to leave your room and walk down the hall to them.

On this fine, brisk early morning, there I was, leaned up against the side of the hallway, directly across from Sam and Chad's door. I was tired and groggy, and could barely see. As I rubbed a booger from my left eye, Sam and Chad's door slowly swung open. I blinked and saw a very casual, slightly pudgy, brown-haired Chad slowly swooping a towel around his naked body, leaving me with a seemingly endless three seconds of full-on boy junk. He looked at me and yawned as he tossed out a "Morning, Eva," then whisked past me and moved on down to the bathroom door, holding nothing but that white towel and a bottle of Axe shower gel.

I was in shock. WTF did I just SEE. Welcome to college!

College classes were different than high school. First of all, you will have to say goodbye to colorful classrooms with personality. No longer will you have the pillars-of-character chart to read when you're zoning out in class. No longer will there be an American flag positioned perfectly over a well-decorated desk filled with eclectic personal mementos belonging to your teacher. No. Instead you will now have a professor, and a bare-walled, popcorn-ceilinged room where there's no assigned seating and the most colorful thing to look at is an art student's personalized knit bag in the corner.

Oh, there are also lecture halls. If you think college is different than high school, wait until you walk through a door you think is going to be a coat closet and instead uncover a 350-seat lecture hall,

where there's literal railings on staircases and you better pick a seat quick before you arrive late and have to literally take a flat-out Great Wall of China hike to find an empty seat.

Okay, now on to the good stuff.

My first college party was, again, just out of a movie. It was a frat party,

TKE. The party was a foam party, and I approached the basement to find a stripper pole and lots of questionable, tepid alcohol in weird clear cups lining a 100 percent moist table of God-knows-what fluids, but most likely spilled drinks. I thought I looked cool, but it took me three more years of college parties to realize that you can always 100,000 percent easily pick out the freshman girls like sore thumbs.

I found a ripped-up red couch and tried not to think of WTF it had seen, and sat there for the rest of the party next to a couple making out and a dreadlocked boy smoking pot. I pulled out my phone and proceeded to call my best friend, Taylor, fighting to hear him over the din of this party in the basement. I needed to at least look *busy*.

Not my thing, right? However, this was not the last college party I went to.

Did college feel like the movies? Honestly? *Yes*.

I remember going out with my friends and seeing movies that would show these insane high school parties. Parties with Christmas lights, kids who lived in enormous mansions by the side of a lake, and fourteen-year-olds that looked like twenty-eight-year-olds (because the actors usually were). That completely warped my idea of high school parties, until I got to

a real high school party and my fantasies were completely diminished. However, college parties, college romances, and college moments honestly felt spot-on to what I'd seen in the movies. Like the time my best friend's bunk bed BROKE on her in the middle of the night. Scene from a movie, right? And I can't tell you how many times this one girl, a roommate of a friend of mine (and who shall remain nameless), broke her thumb practically every night that she went to a party. I mean, I didn't go to the parties. This girl did, and she drank too much. She'd walk around with a little blue thumb cast, and then as soon as it healed, out she'd go and break it all over again.

That made me even more sure that drinking while in college was not for me.

THE BEST THING YOU WILL LEARN IN COLLEGE: *Be Open to Change*

What was the most important thing I learned in college? That it isn't just about figuring out what you like—it's about figuring out what you *don't*.

College is about figuring out what you're good at and what you love and what you can do for your career. Some people start college all sure of what they're going to do, and they stick to the script. Others start and realize after two days that they made a big mistake. It took me a while, but I eventually figured out that I was one of those big-mistakers too. And I'm so glad I did!

I went into college as a broadcast journalism major. I paid for the program and put in the time. I was going to be Oprah. Or I was going to be Katie Couric without the button-down shirts I had worn my junior year of high school. But by the time I was a junior in college, I realized that I hated my major. I was forced to write essays that were so not important to me. I had to sit through lectures I found irrelevant. What clinched it was being flown to New York to do a DIY segment on the *Today* show. How amazing was that! They'd seen me on YouTube and wanted me on network TV!

But then, when I got to the set, it was not glamorous at all. It was tiny and dark and the windows were all closed off and they moved the sets around between segments to make it look bigger. Don't get me wrong—they were very nice to me and it was a fantastic opportunity for exposure, but I found the segment to be out of tune with my quirkier personality, and how I like to get information across on my own videos. It wasn't *me*.

When I got back to college, I figured out that so much of broadcast journalism was all about talking heads who were just puppets who read off teleprompters and talked about topics that few people actually cared out. Yes, they ran important

news stories and did reporting on issues that helped a lot of people. But in between that they were doing human interest stories like how to get the best collar for your kitty at the pet store—and I would have gone nuts doing that! I was already scripting and directing and editing my own videos. I had total control over them. I realized that being in control of my career was the only way to go.

I also figured out that what was really important to my education were all the random classes I had been taking—classes outside my major that sounded fun and interesting and that would take me out of my comfort zone. Some were academic, like biology. I also took an acting class. I did soccer for two years. One of my favorite classes was Ultimate Frisbee. Don't laugh—it was fantastic! Most of my Frisbee classmates were kinesiology majors, and they were really interesting. Another favorite was my debate class. I won every single one because I was really, really good at it. My professor was also the coach of the debate team and tried his best to get me on the team, but I was just too busy with work. I still regret that, because I would have *killed*!

All of these classes ended up being much more "educational" than the courses in my major. Did I need them? No. Did they open my eyes to ideas that stretched me as a thinker and a person? Of course! Did this matter to my parents, and especially my grandpa, who keeps on me about finishing my degree and then going to law school? What do you think LOL?

Can you see me in law school? HA. I do think law is interesting, but it is *so* not happening. But Grandpa keeps nagging. And I want to say, "WTF! Do you know what my career is now? I think I'm making a success of myself, okay? OKAY!"

So don't let your parents push you toward a career that might be lucrative but that you know will make you miserable. Be realistic about job opportunities, because I know it's a jungle out there. But there's nothing worse than wasting your time in college doing something to please somebody else. Trust yourself. You'll figure it out!

COLLEGE . . . AND BOYS . . . AND LOVE

College is also a time for growing up past the drama of high school relationships. One MAJOR thing I learned in college had nothing to do with my classes and everything to do with real life: There are SO. MANY. CRAPPY. GUYS.

Okay, so in high school, there were all these boys that never knew what they were doing when it came to girls, and we played it off by always giving them the excuse that they were "in high school! They're supposed to be idiots!"

But when you get out of high school . . . it turns out that lots of boys are still idiots.

And yet we FALL FOR THEM.

You'd THINK after all the crappy boys I dealt with in high school that I'd have learned tricks to successfully dodge all fukbois from my life. But I haven't. The biggest mistake I always seemed to make was letting someone stay a little too long in my life.

So, what makes boys not be idiots?

A sense of humor. Smarts. Kindness. Responsibility. That, you know, thing that makes your heart beat faster.

Let me tell you about Ethan, who was most definitely not an idiot.

My First Real Adult Relationship

Sophomore year of college came, and I had **just** broken up with a guy named Michael. Like . . . it had been two weeks. Usually in dating, there is this unwritten rule everyone says, which is that we're supposed to "wait a long amount of time before jumping into a new relationship." I believed that fully. I was like, There is NO way I'm going to be "that girl," whatever that meant. I wasn't looking to be tied down again, or find someone new anytime soon.

I was, however, ready to become more independent. I didn't have my driver's license and I **still** lived at home with my parents. I felt this huge urge to grow up. I mean, I was a sophomore in college and was still dependent on my grandma driving me to school every day in the old white van with bread in it. So two weeks passed, and I went on full-on adulting mode. I got my license, dyed my hair black, and even downloaded the Tinder app. (Notice my priorities!) Within a few hundred weird swipes and one awkward Tinder date at a park, I landed on Ethan.

Ethan's profile was charming and witty, and he seemed like just my type. His bio stated, "I'm a dolphin trainer, I have a tattoo on my butt of another man's name, and I ____ (think of something weird and random). Which one is true?" Ethan and I started talking, and it turned out he had a tattoo of Kobe Bryant (no lie) on his right butt cheek. CHEEKY!

We set our first date at a pizza lunch spot so we could casually get to know each other. When I went to pick him up, I was so nervous that when I pulled into the parking space, I accidentally put my car in drive and crashed it into a pole! I had to drive him to the pizza restaurant in a car that could only roll at a pathetic twenty miles an hour while hideous scraping noises were coming out from underneath it. I turned up the radio to tune it out, but that didn't exactly work!

Ethan and I fell in love very quickly. Honestly, it was instant, the first day we met. I just *knew*. A short three weeks later, he asked me to be his girlfriend. He drove me up to the highest hill in the little town we went to school in and got on one knee. He asked me to be his girlfriend while we overlooked the city lights. There I was, fresh out of my old relationship and in a new one, but I wasn't mad about it at all. I was in love.

One week into our deepening relationship, Ethan hesitantly sat me down and told me that on January third, he'd be flying off to Barcelona, Spain, to study abroad for FIVE MONTHS.

He was scared that I wouldn't want to date him anymore, to have a long-distance relationship, because we'd barely even gotten to really know each other for more than a few weeks, even though those few weeks had been amazing. Without hesitation, I knew I wanted to stay with him for however long he'd be away. I told him that he was crazy, that of course we'd stay together, and he was so happy. We both were.

We dated for another amazing month. We attended college parties together, spent Halloween together, studied together in the library. I still remember the feeling I got when I'd get out of class early, walk to the other end of campus, and go into the business building, where his major was, just to wait for him to get out of class. He always had his longboard tucked into his backpack, and sometimes on a really nice day, I'd pull it from him and ride it around next to him when I had a brief moment to hang out with him on campus.

At the time, I was already a YouTuber with around 70,000 subscribers. Christmas season approached, and we had amazing nights decorating his little apartment with multicolored Christmas lights, and had one particularly intense debate about whether the tacks you poked into the wall with colorful ends were called "pushpins" or "thumbtacks." Obviously pushpins—DUH!

The time when he had to leave for Barcelona got closer, and so the day after Christmas, I flew to San Francisco for the first time in my life, alone, to spend time with Ethan and his family before he left. This was the first time I'd ever traveled anywhere that wasn't a trip to see distant family. It was a trip to follow my own heart, which was really scary and made me feel like a total adult.

I slept in Ethan's sister's room, on the bottom bunk, and every day he would show me where he grew up and take me around the city. I only had a few days left with him, and wanted to tell him I loved him before he left for Spain. One night,

as we were driving back to his house, I was so flooded with love that during the entire ride home, I bet him I could tell him a hundred things I loved about him, and I did!

On our last night together, we went to the movies. We went to Starbucks before the film started, and I drew a picture of a plane, Barcelona, and Ethan and me with a heart on a crumpled napkin (you know, to drop those hints). After the movie, we drove home and stopped in the street to look at the stars. In that moment, I felt more alive than I'd ever felt before. There I was, lying next to my boyfriend on the top of the trunk of his old Taurus, gazing up at the sky and thinking about my life.

I certainly wasn't rich, but I made enough to pay for the cheapest one-bedroom college apartment. I didn't have the nicest car—I drove a 1998 Nissan Altima with a huge dent in the side, leather seats, and no aux cord. I wasn't the smartest. I was struggling to get by in most of my classes. But there I was, me, Eva. Someone who had beaten so many odds growing up. Someone who at one point thought her life would be nothing. Someone who at one point felt as if she had nothing to live for.

And then there I was, nineteen years

old, with my life stretching out before me. I had a home, I had a car, I had someone I was madly in love with. I thought about this all and then started to tear up.

Ethan looked at me, looking terribly sad and concerned. He held my face and said, "Why are you crying??? I thought this was a great moment!" I looked at him and wiped the tears from my eyes. Who ever thought I'd be crying because I was so happy? Was that even a thing?

I struggled to find the words to say to him, and felt a little embarrassed admitting such a feeling of euphoria. Although you know by now that I am pretty much an open book, it was still sometimes a struggle for me to get out feelings that were super important and delicate, because I was too fearful of things not sounding perfect. Usually, I wouldn't have said anything profound, but somehow I managed to perfectly get out how I was feeling.

I looked at Ethan. "This is the happiest I've ever felt in my entire life," I said.

He thought about that for a second, then smiled. He knew exactly what I meant.

Of course I began to explain myself, though, because that's just the Eva way. "Look, I know my life isn't amazing and I still have a long way to go and I'm nowhere even close to being put-together

or rich or sexy or famous or successful," I said, rambling through my tears, "but in this moment, right here, in this spot that my life is right now . . . my life feels perfect."

"I love you," Ethan said. And he started to tear up too.

That was the most beautiful moment I ever felt.

Ethan flew to Barcelona the next day, and I flew back home. I didn't see him for four very long months. By the fifth month, my grandparents helped me get me a passport and I flew for the first time overseas, on my own. We were so happy to see each other, and our relationship was amazing. That was only the start. We traveled together to foreign countries. I rode my first motorcycle with him. I even rode my first elephant with him! He saw me go from Eva Gutowski, a nineteen-year-old girl with a fun little YouTube channel, to MyLifeAsEva, a two-million-subscriber businesswoman. He had been with me during what was the biggest change in my life. He had loved me before MyLifeAsEva. And everything was great.

Until we both just started drifting apart.

There came a point where Ethan and I were at a crossroads in both our lives. He was graduating from college, was always studying, and had dreams of living in Germany and working in other countries. I was moving to Los Angeles and was never home. I'd dyed my hair blond, which Ethan hated, and bought a 2009 used BMW convertible. We were both changing, becoming different people. Actually, we were both just growing up.

We tried to stay together for as long as possible, but eventually ended things when it got too hard. The problem was, we still loved each other so damn much. We just were going in completely different directions and had different goals for ourselves in different careers and different cities, and didn't know what to do anymore. Months went by where we'd try to work things out, and it became really emotionally tiring. I wanted to marry Ethan with all my heart, butt, and soul. He was it. He was my other half!

It's insane when you go your whole life thinking that "settling down" is this distant fantasy that one day you'll figure out . . . and then you find someone that you fall madly in love with, who is your best friend, understands you and your goofy humor like no one else had, helps you recognize and deal with your deepest issues . . . and then it just fizzles out and ends—it's unbelievably hard and painful.

I had no doubt that Ethan was my soul mate, and then time went on and it didn't seem so much like that was true anymore.

TBH, the hardest part is putting so much effort into one person and thinking all the time and love and care spent is going to be worth it when you spend the rest of your life together, but then it's over, and you're tired because you've fought so hard to keep it together, and then it hits you that, damn, Eva, you've just invested so much time of your life loving this person so damn hard and it's all over . . . and now you're going to have to do that all again, just for it to maybe never amount to ending well.

That part really sucks, but I just had to tell myself that and realize that not everyone in your life is meant to be in your life forever.

In fact, 95 percent of people you meet will only be in your life for a minor amount of time, and most will never occupy important roles. The few people who come and go as your best friend, or who come and go as someone you fall in love with, are all meant to help you to learn the art of trial and error, of growing up and understanding people better and more truly. It's about realizing that you're sometimes going to be loving someone for the memories and what they've taught you, instead of you resenting someone for not sticking around. If we got caught up in people leaving our lives all the time, we'd go crazy!

Life is not about how many friends or

people you love or who you grow apart from. It's about them all being a part of the amazing and many chapters that life has. I'll be the first to be proud to say that if Ethan and I hadn't broken up, I would have never reached my full potential of satisfaction with life.

At the time that Ethan and I were super serious, there was still so much more in life I hadn't done, and I knew deep down that Ethan was not the ideal person I needed to do those things with. As many similarities as we had, Ethan was also very different in his attitude toward things I desperately needed him to be in tune with me on.

After we split, I finally took up surfing, which was something I had dreamed of being good at since I was eleven years old! I took up making music. I hiked and felt the wind on my face in parts of the world I had once been too afraid to reach. I did things the spontaneous, natural way, not the planned way. I experienced living on a completely new level—and all of these things only happened because I realized my life was in my own hands, not in the hands of someone else.

If I had stayed with Ethan, I would NEVER have learned so many things! Like, did you know that in some of the clubs in Los Angeles, they have a lady sitting in the bathroom JUST to help you wash your hands? Or that if you spray yourself with bug spray, you'll get a shiny glow like a Victoria's Secret model? Or that if you put Cup Noodles in the microwave with no water, it'll catch fire and blow up??! (Seriously, it happened. I know I told you this already, but it is so worth repeating: Do NOT try this at home, kids!)

Most of all, I recognized that I was too young at heart and soul—and this is true no matter what your age—to be compromising my dreams to settle with another. I needed to go through a real adult love affair and real adult breakup to fully understand that.

Ethan and I loved each other like crazy, but we both had to learn how loving someone does not always mean staying with them forever. Lots of times love can shift meaning, and that's all a part of life. Ethan and I wished the best for each other, and he will always have a special place in my heart. Moving on from relationships that seemed like they would last forever is hard, but it's not impossible. I thought back to how I got over having some of my besties hurt me so much, and I followed my own advice. My life is so much more fulfilled now.

And I know my soul mate is out there, and believe me, I'll be ready.

SEE THE

WORLD

NOW

CHAPTER 14

Glo-Up Level, ME NOW

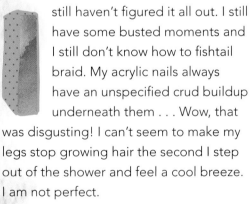

still haven't figured it all out. I still have some busted moments and I still don't know how to fishtail braid. My acrylic nails always have an unspecified crud buildup underneath them . . . Wow, that was disgusting! I can't seem to make my legs stop growing hair the second I step out of the shower and feel a cool breeze. I am not perfect.

But that's the point.

We're not supposed to have it all figured out. Even the people who seem like they have it all figured out, don't. Not really.

It's so funny, because I've grown up my whole life with this weird thing that happens to the back of my legs, where the skin is always dry, bumpy, and itchy. I'd have good days where my legs would seem soft and smooth, and most days where my legs would seem like sandpaper. Nonetheless, I could never seem to get rid of this bumpiness, and I still can't. I have tons of scars all over my legs from falling a million times, and I have a giant birthmark on my butt that looks like a dirt stain and is oddly shaped like a rubber duck holding an umbrella. My legs are rarely EVER shaven. I'm not one of those girls that shaves twice a week. I don't have time for that. Seriously, I shave once every like eight days if I HAVE to. Back when I danced in high school, I'd

only shave my legs so girls would stop petting them when we stretched before class. Literally, my legs were petted when it was shorts season.

I have acne scars all over my face that I can't seem to get to fade away, and some days they are more red and some days they are more faded. My skin is super dry and I don't drink enough water.

I cry sometimes. I go through hard moments. People break my heart. My parents stress me out. My future stresses me out. Some days I feel like *if nothing is wrong, why am I so unhappy?*

But then I see a picture of me in a bikini on some random beach, and I think, Oh my God, you can't even notice!

My legs look flawless! The hair can't even be seen! My acne scars are blended in! The twelve-megapixel quality completely takes away all my flaws! My birthmark is faded into my tan! And no one can even tell I was crying the night before about some boy that hurt me.

You see pictures, and you think, Wow, this person is perfect, but in fact, there's a lot hiding from a photo, even if we don't even mean to hide it!

I don't airbrush myself, and I don't Facetune my boobs to be a few sizes bigger. I don't try to fake being a perfect human, but sometimes great photos are taken and posted and you don't even realize all there is to the person behind the photo.

We don't wake up looking perfect, and if you lived in any person's shoes for a week, you'd realize it's not just you that has flaws . . . because we ALL do. Think about when you touch the inside of your belly button and smell it and think, Wow, I must be pretty disgusting. Guess what? Everyone's belly button smells like that. Trust me, I've done research.

I still haven't figured out how to be perfect, and I doubt I ever will, and honestly, I don't really want to find out. Being perfect looks like it takes too much work. I mean, seriously, if I can't even handle shaving my legs three times a month, how the hell am I going to juggle being perfect in every way?

I think the important thing to remember in this world where we're all striving to be SOMETHING is don't strive to be perfect. Don't strive to perfect every little thing you think you're doing wrong and someone else is doing right. It's perfectly okay to want to know how to do this best or that best, but to get caught up in something always being "less than" on you is toxic.

Just be yourself.

That's what I'm doing. Everything good and bad and silly and crazy and messed up and weird . . . and loving and kind and generous and hopeful. That's what gave me the strength to forgive. That's what gave me the courage to become a YouTuber. That's what gave me, Eva, the opportunity to write this book, even though I kind of took a few, *um*, shortcuts in English class in high school!

That's what gave me the ability to be fully and completely myself.

So . . . what are you waiting for?

It's time for you to live your life as YOU! The world can seem like a really scary, waaaaay-too-big place, but I want you to know that there **is** a place in this world that's just for **you**, and it's waiting for you to discover it.

Go out there and make every single one of your dreams come true.

I can't wait to see them all happen for you, and I hope this book will be there for you . . . every step of the way!

Acknowledgments

I want to thank my amazing managers, Scott Fisher and Adam Wescott, for taking me under their wing at the start of my YouTube career and seeing my potential before anyone else did. Because you believed in me, I got to live out my wildest dreams and continue to dream bigger every day. Thanks also to Caroline Nardilla; my agent, Steve Troha; my editor, Natasha Simons; my publicist, Stephanie DeLuca; and my publisher, Jen Bergstrom.

For Karen Moline, thank you for inspiring me every day, for sharing artistic lattes with me in New York hotel cafes, for giving me life advice while we should have been working, and for helping me with what is the most important thing I've ever worked on. You're an amazing partner and friend to me.

To my best friends, thank you so much for showing me what care and compassion look like. Thank you for showing me what a shoulder to cry on feels like, thank you for going to weird naked spas in downtown LA with me, and thank you for always filling me with laughter and love each and every day.

To my family, thank you for shaping me into such a strong and passionate girl. I wouldn't trade a second of my life for anything else. You gave me the things that continue to make me me. From dance to drama to that expensive and kind of pointless eighth-grade school trip to Washington, DC, I appreciate everything you've done for me and love you so much. Thank you thank you thank you.

Image Credits

Courtesy of the author: pgs. ii, iii, iv, vi, 10, 26, 27, 29, 31, 34, 35, 36, 52, 72, 74, 80, 83, 85, 100, 101, 102, 103, 104, 115, 121, 126, 133, 138, 154, 168, 170, 171, 172, 173, 174, 176, 179, 185, 188, 189, 192, 196, 198

© Andrew Stiles: pgs. 8, 9, 22, 23, 24, 25, 70, 71, 77, 78, 79, 118, 119, 122, 123, 126, 128, 129, 130, 131, 132, 140, 152, 153, 165, 166, 167, 190, 191

Illustrations by Jane Archer

pg. v: Illustrations of Eva; pg. 1: Dropcap; pgs. 4–5: Handlettering; pgs. 8–9: Word drawings, tribal pattern; pg. 10: Word drawing; pgs. 22–23: Word drawings; pg. 25: Dropcap; pgs. 36–37: Heart doodle, flower and leaves; pg. 70: Daisies; pg. 72: "E" pattern; pg. 78: Word drawing; pg. 80: Flowers; pg. 81: Tribal pattern; pg. 95: Word drawing; pg. 100: Flower; pg. 107: Watercolor art; pgs. 116–117: Vegetables, soup, handlettering; pgs. 118–119: Eva's News sticker, boots pattern, coffee, swirly "E"; pgs. 122–123: Flower, handlettering; pgs. 128–129: Handlettering; pg. 132: Wifi graphic; pg. 133: Dropcap; pg. 141: Dropcap; pgs. 152–153: Popcorn sticker, ice-pop pattern; pg. 155: Dropcap; pg. 164: Dolphin; pgs. 166–167: Sea otter, Paris sticker, palm trees, yellow flower; pg. 170: Handlettering; pg. 171: "E" pattern; pg. 172: Tropical flower; pg. 174: Tropical flower; pg. 175: Dropcap; pg. 190: Flowers, handlettering; pg. 195: Handlettering

All other illustrations from Shutterstock.